I WRITE
...because my story matters.

THE WRITER CRUSHING 2022 IS:

_____

2022 - 2023

I Write 2022 Author Planner
Copyright © 2021 by Dana Pittman.

All rights reserved.

Published by: Purpose Prevails Publishing
2231B Center St STE 144
Deer Park, TX 77536
www.purposeprevailspublishing.com

ISBN-13: 978-1-950405-18-3 (Paperback). *Bestseller*.
ISBN-13: 978-1-950405-19-0 (Paperback). *Dream Catcher*.
ISBN-13: 978-1-950405-20-6 (Paperback). *Sweet Thorns*.
ISBN-13: 978-1-950405-33-6 (Paperback). *Storyteller*.
ISBN-13: 978-1-950405-34-3 (Paperback). *Color My World*.

Designed by Dana Pittman.

I Write Author Planner is available in hardback (limited edition) paperback, printable, and digital formats. There is a companion course to get your started, as well. For more information visit www.iwriteplanner.com.

No part of this book may be reproduced in any form or by any electronic or mechanical means, including information storage and retrieval systems, without written permission from the author, except for the use of brief quotations in a book review.

For more information or group discounts visit www.iwriteplanner.com.

Your story and your voice matters. So, don't just think about your book. Write it!

— DANA PITTMAN
Chief Storyteller with Danja Tales

2022

JANUARY

	S	M	T	W	T	F	S
W52							1
W1	2	3	4	5	6	7	8
W2	9	10	11	12	13	14	15
W3	16	17	18	19	20	21	22
W4	23	24	25	26	27	28	29
W5	30	31					

FEBRUARY

	S	M	T	W	T	F	S
W5			1	2	3	4	5
W6	6	7	8	9	10	11	12
W7	13	14	15	16	17	18	19
W8	20	21	22	23	24	25	26
W9	27	28					

MARCH

	S	M	T	W	T	F	S
W9			1	2	3	4	5
W10	6	7	8	9	10	11	12
W11	13	14	15	16	17	18	19
W12	20	21	22	23	24	25	26
W13	27	28	29	30	31		

APRIL

	S	M	T	W	T	F	S
W13						1	2
W14	3	4	5	6	7	8	9
W15	10	11	12	13	14	15	16
W16	17	18	19	20	21	22	23
W17	24	25	26	27	28	29	30

MAY

	S	M	T	W	T	F	S
W18	1	2	3	4	5	6	7
W19	8	9	10	11	12	13	14
W20	15	16	17	18	19	20	21
W21	22	23	24	25	26	27	28
W22	29	30	31				

JUNE

	S	M	T	W	T	F	S
W22				1	2	3	4
W23	5	6	7	8	9	10	11
W24	12	13	14	15	16	17	18
W25	19	20	21	22	23	24	25
W26	26	27	28	29	30		

JULY

	S	M	T	W	T	F	S
W26						1	2
W27	3	4	5	6	7	8	9
W28	10	11	12	13	14	15	16
W29	17	18	19	20	21	22	23
W30	24	25	26	27	28	29	30
W31	31						

AUGUST

	S	M	T	W	T	F	S
W31		1	2	3	4	5	6
W32	7	8	9	10	11	12	13
W33	14	15	16	17	18	19	20
W34	21	22	23	24	25	26	27
W35	28	29	30	31			

SEPTEMBER

	S	M	T	W	T	F	S
W35					1	2	3
W36	4	5	6	7	8	9	10
W37	11	12	13	14	15	16	17
W38	18	19	20	21	22	23	24
W39	25	26	27	28	29	30	

OCTOBER

	S	M	T	W	T	F	S
W39							1
W40	2	3	4	5	6	7	8
W41	9	10	11	12	13	14	15
W42	16	17	18	19	20	21	22
W43	23	24	25	26	27	28	29
W44	30	31					

NOVEMBER

	S	M	T	W	T	F	S
W44			1	2	3	4	5
W45	6	7	8	9	10	11	12
W46	13	14	15	16	17	18	19
W47	20	21	22	23	24	25	26
W48	27	28	29	30			

DECEMBER

	S	M	T	W	T	F	S
W48					1	2	3
W49	4	5	6	7	8	9	10
W50	11	12	13	14	15	16	17
W51	18	19	20	21	22	23	24
W52	25	26	27	28	29	30	31

2023

JANUARY
	S	M	T	W	T	F	S
W1		1	2	3	4	5	6	7
W2	8	9	10	11	12	13	14
W3	15	16	17	18	19	20	21
W4	22	23	24	25	26	27	28
W5	29	30	31				

FEBRUARY
	S	M	T	W	T	F	S
W5				1	2	3	4
W6	5	6	7	8	9	10	11
W7	12	13	14	15	16	17	18
W8	19	20	21	22	23	24	25
W9	26	27	28				

MARCH
	S	M	T	W	T	F	S
W9				1	2	3	4
W10	5	6	7	8	9	10	11
W11	12	13	14	15	16	17	18
W12	19	20	21	22	23	24	25
W13	26	27	28	29	30	31	

APRIL
	S	M	T	W	T	F	S
W13							1
W14	2	3	4	5	6	7	8
W15	9	10	11	12	13	14	15
W16	16	17	18	19	20	21	22
W17	23	24	25	26	27	28	29
W18	30						

MAY
	S	M	T	W	T	F	S
W18		1	2	3	4	5	6
W19	7	8	9	10	11	12	13
W20	14	15	16	17	18	19	20
W21	21	22	23	24	25	26	27
W22	28	29	30	31			

JUNE
	S	M	T	W	T	F	S
W22					1	2	3
W23	4	5	6	7	8	9	10
W24	11	12	13	14	15	16	17
W25	18	19	20	21	22	23	24
W26	25	26	27	28	29	30	

JULY
	S	M	T	W	T	F	S
W26							1
W27	2	3	4	5	6	7	8
W28	9	10	11	12	13	14	15
W29	16	17	18	19	20	21	22
W30	23	24	25	26	27	28	29
W31	30	31					

AUGUST
	S	M	T	W	T	F	S
W31			1	2	3	4	5
W32	6	7	8	9	10	11	12
W33	13	14	15	16	17	18	19
W34	20	21	22	23	24	25	26
W35	27	28	29	30	31		

SEPTEMBER
	S	M	T	W	T	F	S
W35						1	2
W36	3	4	5	6	7	8	9
W37	10	11	12	13	14	15	16
W38	17	18	19	20	21	22	23
W39	24	25	26	27	28	29	30

OCTOBER
	S	M	T	W	T	F	S
W40	1	2	3	4	5	6	7
W41	8	9	10	11	12	13	14
W42	15	16	17	18	19	20	21
W43	22	23	24	25	26	27	28
W44	29	30	31				

NOVEMBER
	S	M	T	W	T	F	S
W44				1	2	3	4
W45	5	6	7	8	9	10	11
W46	12	13	14	15	16	17	18
W47	19	20	21	22	23	24	25
W48	26	27	28	29	30		

DECEMBER
	S	M	T	W	T	F	S
W48						1	2
W49	3	4	5	6	7	8	9
W50	10	11	12	13	14	15	16
W51	17	18	19	20	21	22	23
W52	24	25	26	27	28	29	30
W1	31						

FUTURE LOG
2022

JANUARY
	S	M	T	W	T	F	S
W52							1
W1	2	3	4	5	6	7	8
W2	9	10	11	12	13	14	15
W3	16	17	18	19	20	21	22
W4	23	24	25	26	27	28	29
W5	30	31					

FEBRUARY
	S	M	T	W	T	F	S
W5			1	2	3	4	5
W6	6	7	8	9	10	11	12
W7	13	14	15	16	17	18	19
W8	20	21	22	23	24	25	26
W9	27	28					

MARCH
	S	M	T	W	T	F	S
W9			1	2	3	4	5
W10	6	7	8	9	10	11	12
W11	13	14	15	16	17	18	19
W12	20	21	22	23	24	25	26
W13	27	28	29	30	31		

_____
_____
_____
_____
_____

APRIL
	S	M	T	W	T	F	S
W13						1	2
W14	3	4	5	6	7	8	9
W15	10	11	12	13	14	15	16
W16	17	18	19	20	21	22	23
W17	24	25	26	27	28	29	30

MAY
	S	M	T	W	T	F	S
W18	1	2	3	4	5	6	7
W19	8	9	10	11	12	13	14
W20	15	16	17	18	19	20	21
W21	22	23	24	25	26	27	28
W22	29	30	31				

JUNE
	S	M	T	W	T	F	S
W22				1	2	3	4
W23	5	6	7	8	9	10	11
W24	12	13	14	15	16	17	18
W25	19	20	21	22	23	24	25
W26	26	27	28	29	30		

_____
_____
_____
_____
_____

FUTURE LOG
2022

JULY
	S	M	T	W	T	F	S
W26						1	2
W27	3	4	5	6	7	8	9
W28	10	11	12	13	14	15	16
W29	17	18	19	20	21	22	23
W30	24	25	26	27	28	29	30
W31	31						

AUGUST
	S	M	T	W	T	F	S
W31		1	2	3	4	5	6
W32	7	8	9	10	11	12	13
W33	14	15	16	17	18	19	20
W34	21	22	23	24	25	26	27
W35	28	29	30	31			

SEPTEMBER
	S	M	T	W	T	F	S
W35					1	2	3
W36	4	5	6	7	8	9	10
W37	11	12	13	14	15	16	17
W38	18	19	20	21	22	23	24
W39	25	26	27	28	29	30	

OCTOBER
	S	M	T	W	T	F	S
W39							1
W40	2	3	4	5	6	7	8
W41	9	10	11	12	13	14	15
W42	16	17	18	19	20	21	22
W43	23	24	25	26	27	28	29
W44	30	31					

NOVEMBER
	S	M	T	W	T	F	S
W44			1	2	3	4	5
W45	6	7	8	9	10	11	12
W46	13	14	15	16	17	18	19
W47	20	21	22	23	24	25	26
W48	27	28	29	30			

DECEMBER
	S	M	T	W	T	F	S
W48					1	2	3
W49	4	5	6	7	8	9	10
W50	11	12	13	14	15	16	17
W51	18	19	20	21	22	23	24
W52	25	26	27	28	29	30	31

WRITING SNAPSHOT
2022

JANUARY

	S	M	T	W	T	F	S
W52							1
W1	2	3	4	5	6	7	8
W2	9	10	11	12	13	14	15
W3	16	17	18	19	20	21	22
W4	23	24	25	26	27	28	29
W5	30	31					

FEBRUARY

	S	M	T	W	T	F	S
W5			1	2	3	4	5
W6	6	7	8	9	10	11	12
W7	13	14	15	16	17	18	19
W8	20	21	22	23	24	25	26
W9	27	28					

MARCH

	S	M	T	W	T	F	S
W9			1	2	3	4	5
W10	6	7	8	9	10	11	12
W11	13	14	15	16	17	18	19
W12	20	21	22	23	24	25	26
W13	27	28	29	30	31		

APRIL

	S	M	T	W	T	F	S
W13						1	2
W14	3	4	5	6	7	8	9
W15	10	11	12	13	14	15	16
W16	17	18	19	20	21	22	23
W17	24	25	26	27	28	29	30

MAY

	S	M	T	W	T	F	S
W18	1	2	3	4	5	6	7
W19	8	9	10	11	12	13	14
W20	15	16	17	18	19	20	21
W21	22	23	24	25	26	27	28
W22	29	30	31				

JUNE

	S	M	T	W	T	F	S
W22				1	2	3	4
W23	5	6	7	8	9	10	11
W24	12	13	14	15	16	17	18
W25	19	20	21	22	23	24	25
W26	26	27	28	29	30		

WRITING SNAPSHOT
2022

JULY

	S	M	T	W	T	F	S
W26						1	2
W27	3	4	5	6	7	8	9
W28	10	11	12	13	14	15	16
W29	17	18	19	20	21	22	23
W30	24	25	26	27	28	29	30
W31	31						

AUGUST

	S	M	T	W	T	F	S
W31		1	2	3	4	5	6
W32	7	8	9	10	11	12	13
W33	14	15	16	17	18	19	20
W34	21	22	23	24	25	26	27
W35	28	29	30	31			

SEPTEMBER

	S	M	T	W	T	F	S
W35					1	2	3
W36	4	5	6	7	8	9	10
W37	11	12	13	14	15	16	17
W38	18	19	20	21	22	23	24
W39	25	26	27	28	29	30	

_____

_____

_____

_____

OCTOBER

	S	M	T	W	T	F	S
W39							1
W40	2	3	4	5	6	7	8
W41	9	10	11	12	13	14	15
W42	16	17	18	19	20	21	22
W43	23	24	25	26	27	28	29
W44	30	31					

NOVEMBER

	S	M	T	W	T	F	S
W44			1	2	3	4	5
W45	6	7	8	9	10	11	12
W46	13	14	15	16	17	18	19
W47	20	21	22	23	24	25	26
W48	27	28	29	30			

DECEMBER

	S	M	T	W	T	F	S
W48					1	2	3
W49	4	5	6	7	8	9	10
W50	11	12	13	14	15	16	17
W51	18	19	20	21	22	23	24
W52	25	26	27	28	29	30	31

_____

_____

_____

_____

MARKETING SNAPSHOT
2022

JANUARY

BOOKS:
SUBSCRIBERS:
FB FOLLOWERS:
IG FOLLOWERS:
TWITTER FOLLOWERS:
FOLLOWERS:
FOLLOWERS:

NOTES

FEBRUARY

BOOKS:
SUBSCRIBERS:
FB FOLLOWERS:
IG FOLLOWERS:
TWITTER FOLLOWERS:
FOLLOWERS:
FOLLOWERS:

NOTES

MARCH

BOOKS:
SUBSCRIBERS:
FB FOLLOWERS:
IG FOLLOWERS:
TWITTER FOLLOWERS:
FOLLOWERS:
FOLLOWERS:

NOTES

APRIL

BOOKS:
SUBSCRIBERS:
FB FOLLOWERS:
IG FOLLOWERS:
TWITTER FOLLOWERS:
FOLLOWERS:
FOLLOWERS:

NOTES

MAY

BOOKS:
SUBSCRIBERS:
FB FOLLOWERS:
IG FOLLOWERS:
TWITTER FOLLOWERS:
FOLLOWERS:
FOLLOWERS:

NOTES

JUNE

BOOKS:
SUBSCRIBERS:
FB FOLLOWERS:
IG FOLLOWERS:
TWITTER FOLLOWERS:
FOLLOWERS:
FOLLOWERS:

NOTES

MARKETING SNAPSHOT
2022

JULY

BOOKS:

SUBSCRIBERS:

FB FOLLOWERS:

IG FOLLOWERS:

TWITTER FOLLOWERS:

FOLLOWERS:

FOLLOWERS:

NOTES

AUGUST

BOOKS:

SUBSCRIBERS:

FB FOLLOWERS:

IG FOLLOWERS:

TWITTER FOLLOWERS:

FOLLOWERS:

FOLLOWERS:

NOTES

SEPTEMBER

BOOKS:

SUBSCRIBERS:

FB FOLLOWERS:

IG FOLLOWERS:

TWITTER FOLLOWERS:

FOLLOWERS:

FOLLOWERS:

NOTES

OCTOBER

BOOKS:

SUBSCRIBERS:

FB FOLLOWERS:

IG FOLLOWERS:

TWITTER FOLLOWERS:

FOLLOWERS:

FOLLOWERS:

NOTES

NOVEMBER

BOOKS:

SUBSCRIBERS:

FB FOLLOWERS:

IG FOLLOWERS:

TWITTER FOLLOWERS:

FOLLOWERS:

FOLLOWERS:

NOTES

DECEMBER

BOOKS:

SUBSCRIBERS:

FB FOLLOWERS:

IG FOLLOWERS:

TWITTER FOLLOWERS:

FOLLOWERS:

FOLLOWERS:

NOTES

FINANCIAL SNAPSHOT
2022

JANUARY

GOAL:

INCOME:

EXPENSES:

NET:

NOTES

FEBRUARY

GOAL:

INCOME:

EXPENSES:

NET:

NOTES

MARCH

GOAL:

INCOME:

EXPENSES:

NET:

NOTES

APRIL

GOAL:

INCOME:

EXPENSES:

NET:

NOTES

MAY

GOAL:

INCOME:

EXPENSES:

NET:

NOTES

JUNE

GOAL:

INCOME:

EXPENSES:

NET:

NOTES

FINANCIAL SNAPSHOT
2022

JULY

GOAL:

INCOME:

EXPENSES:

NET:

NOTES

AUGUST

GOAL:

INCOME:

EXPENSES:

NET:

NOTES

SEPTEMBER

GOAL:

INCOME:

EXPENSES:

NET:

NOTES

OCTOBER

GOAL:

INCOME:

EXPENSES:

NET:

NOTES

NOVEMBER

GOAL:

INCOME:

EXPENSES:

NET:

NOTES

DECEMBER

GOAL:

INCOME:

EXPENSES:

NET:

NOTES

...my story matters.

JANUARY 2022

JANUARY
2022

FOCUS:

NOTES	SUNDAY	MONDAY	TUESDAY
	WEEK 52		
	2 / WEEK 1	3	4
	9 / WEEK 2	10	11
	16 / WEEK 3	17	18
	23 / WEEK 4 / 30	24 / 31	25

	SU MO TU WE TH FR SA		SU MO TU WE TH FR SA
DECEMBER W48	1 2 3 4	FEBRUARY W5	1 2 3 4 5
W49	5 6 7 8 9 10 11	W6	6 7 8 9 10 11 12
W50	12 13 14 15 16 17 18	W7	13 14 15 16 17 18 19
W51	19 20 21 22 23 24 25	W8	20 21 22 23 24 25 26
W52	26 27 28 29 30 31	W9	27 28

WEDNESDAY	THURSDAY	FRIDAY	SATURDAY
			1
5	6	7	8
12	13	14	15
19	20	21	22
27	28	29	30

JANUARY
OVERVIEW

FOCUS:

REMINDERS

GOAL

GOAL

THINGS TO REMEMBER

- ☐
- ☐
- ☐
- ☐
- ☐
- ☐
- ☐
- ☐
- ☐
- ☐
- ☐
- ☐

GOAL

GOAL

Master To Do List

- [ ]
- [ ] _____ Due Date _____
- [ ] _____ Due Date _____
- [ ] _____ Due Date _____
- [ ] _____ Due Date _____
- [ ] _____ Due Date _____
- [ ] _____ Due Date _____
- [ ] _____ Due Date _____
- [ ] _____ Due Date _____
- [ ] _____ Due Date _____
- [ ] _____ Due Date _____
- [ ] _____ Due Date _____
- [ ] _____ Due Date _____
- [ ] _____ Due Date _____
- [ ] _____ Due Date _____
- [ ] _____ Due Date _____
- [ ] _____ Due Date _____
- [ ] _____ Due Date _____
- [ ] _____ Due Date _____
- [ ] _____ Due Date _____
- [ ] _____ Due Date _____
- [ ] _____ Due Date _____
- [ ] _____ Due Date _____
- [ ] _____ Due Date _____

WORD COUNT TRACKER

GOAL FOR THIS MONTH	I ACHIEVED

YEAR TO DATE: _____

FOCUS THIS WEEK:

WEEK 52 — DECEMBER 26 – JANUARY 1

TOP PRIORITIES — APPOINTMENTS / DEADLINES

WRITING:

MARKETING — NOTES

LIST SOMETHING GOOD FROM THIS WEEK.

LIST HOW YOU CAN MAKE NEXT WEEK BETTER.

	SU	MO	TU	WE	TH	FR	SA
W52	26	27	28	29	30	31	1
W1	2	3	4	5	6	7	8
W2	9	10	11	12	13	14	15
W3	16	17	18	19	20	21	22
W4	23	24	25	26	27	28	29
W5	30	31					

JANUARY

SUNDAY | 26

MONDAY | 27

TUESDAY | 28

WEDNESDAY | 29

THURSDAY | 30

FRIDAY | 31

SATURDAY | 01

REMEMBER FOR NEXT WEEK

WRITING THIS WEEK

WEEK 52   DECEMBER 26 – JANUARY 1

What I'm writing this week? And how will I measure it (words, scenes, etc)?

When will I get it done?

What do I need to make it happen?

What could keep me from reaching my goal?

How'd I do? Did I reach my goal? Exceed my goal? Miss my goal?

What can I change next week to improve my outcome?

Do I need assistance to make it happen? If so, who?

FOCUS THIS WEEK:

WEEK 1   JANUARY 2 – JANUARY 8

TOP PRIORITIES	APPOINTMENTS / DEADLINES
	/
	/
	/
	/
	/
	/

WRITING:

MARKETING   **NOTES**

LIST SOMETHING GOOD FROM THIS WEEK.   LIST HOW YOU CAN MAKE NEXT WEEK BETTER.

	SU	MO	TU	WE	TH	FR	SA
W52							1
W1	2	3	4	5	6	7	8
W2	9	10	11	12	13	14	15
W3	16	17	18	19	20	21	22
W4	23	24	25	26	27	28	29
W5	30	31					

JANUARY

SUNDAY | 02

MONDAY | 03

TUESDAY | 04

WEDNESDAY | 05

THURSDAY | 06

FRIDAY | 07

SATURDAY | 08

REMEMBER FOR NEXT WEEK

WRITING THIS WEEK

WEEK 1   JANUARY 2 – JANUARY 8

What I'm writing this week? And how will I measure it (words, scenes, etc)?

When will I get it done?

What do I need to make it happen?

What could keep me from reaching my goal?

How'd I do? Did I reach my goal? Exceed my goal? Miss my goal?

What can I change next week to improve my outcome?

Do I need assistance to make it happen? If so, who?

FOCUS THIS WEEK:

WEEK 2 JANUARY 9 – JANUARY 15

TOP PRIORITIES APPOINTMENTS / DEADLINES

/
/
/
/
/
/

WRITING:

MARKETING **NOTES**

LIST SOMETHING GOOD FROM THIS WEEK. LIST HOW YOU CAN MAKE NEXT WEEK BETTER.

	SU	MO	TU	WE	TH	FR	SA
W52							1
W1	2	3	4	5	6	7	8
W2	9	10	11	12	13	14	15
W3	16	17	18	19	20	21	22
W4	23	24	25	26	27	28	29
W5	30	31					

JANUARY

SUNDAY | 09

MONDAY | 10

TUESDAY | 11

WEDNESDAY | 12

THURSDAY | 13

FRIDAY | 14

SATURDAY | 15

REMEMBER FOR NEXT WEEK

WRITING THIS WEEK

WEEK 2   JANUARY 9 – JANUARY 15

What I'm writing this week? And how will I measure it (words, scenes, etc)?

When will I get it done?

What do I need to make it happen?

What could keep me from reaching my goal?

How'd I do? Did I reach my goal? Exceed my goal? Miss my goal?

What can I change next week to improve my outcome?

Do I need assistance to make it happen? If so, who?

FOCUS THIS WEEK:

WEEK 3   JANUARY 16 – JANUARY 22

TOP PRIORITIES

APPOINTMENTS / DEADLINES

/
/
/
/
/
/

WRITING:

MARKETING

NOTES

LIST SOMETHING GOOD FROM THIS WEEK.

LIST HOW YOU CAN MAKE NEXT WEEK BETTER.

	SU	MO	TU	WE	TH	FR	SA
W52							1
W1	2	3	4	5	6	7	8
W2	9	10	11	12	13	14	15
W3	16	17	18	19	20	21	22
W4	23	24	25	26	27	28	29
W5	30	31					

JANUARY

SUNDAY | 16

MONDAY | 17

TUESDAY | 18

WEDNESDAY | 19

THURSDAY | 20

FRIDAY | 21

SATURDAY | 22

REMEMBER FOR NEXT WEEK

WRITING THIS WEEK

WEEK 3   JANUARY 16 – JANUARY 22

What I'm writing this week? And how will I measure it (words, scenes, etc)?

When will I get it done?

What do I need to make it happen?

What could keep me from reaching my goal?

How'd I do? Did I reach my goal? Exceed my goal? Miss my goal?

What can I change next week to improve my outcome?

Do I need assistance to make it happen? If so, who?

FOCUS THIS WEEK:

WEEK 4 　　　　　　　　　　　　　　　　　　　　　　　　　　　　　　　　JANUARY 23 – JANUARY 29

TOP PRIORITIES　　　　　　　　　APPOINTMENTS / DEADLINES

/
/
/
/
/
/

WRITING:

MARKETING　　　　　　　　　　　　　　　　NOTES

LIST SOMETHING GOOD FROM THIS WEEK.　　　　LIST HOW YOU CAN MAKE NEXT WEEK BETTER.

	SU	MO	TU	WE	TH	FR	SA
W52							1
W1	2	3	4	5	6	7	8
W2	9	10	11	12	13	14	15
W3	16	17	18	19	20	21	22
W4	23	24	25	26	27	28	29
W5	30	31					

JANUARY

SUNDAY | 23

MONDAY | 24

TUESDAY | 25

WEDNESDAY | 26

THURSDAY | 27

FRIDAY | 28

SATURDAY | 29

REMEMBER FOR NEXT WEEK

WRITING THIS WEEK

WEEK 4   JANUARY 23 – JANUARY 29

What I'm writing this week? And how will I measure it (words, scenes, etc)?

When will I get it done?

What do I need to make it happen?

What could keep me from reaching my goal?

How'd I do? Did I reach my goal? Exceed my goal? Miss my goal?

What can I change next week to improve my outcome?

Do I need assistance to make it happen? If so, who?

JANUARY
REVIEW

MY GOALS FOR THIS MONTH:
_____
_____
_____
_____
_____
_____

THIS MONTH I ACHIEVED:
_____
_____
_____
_____

WHAT WORKED:
_____
_____
_____
_____

WHAT DIDN'T WORK:
_____
_____
_____

DO MORE OF:	DO LESS OF:
_____	_____
_____	_____
_____	_____
_____	_____
_____	_____

INCOME TRACKER

GOAL FOR THIS MONTH	I ACHIEVED

Date	Source	Description	Amount
	TOTAL INCOME		

EXPENSE TRACKER

GOAL FOR THIS MONTH	I ACHIEVED

Date	Category	Description	Amount
		TOTAL EXPENSES	

...my story matters.

FEBRUARY 2022

FEBRUARY
2022

FOCUS:

NOTES	SUNDAY	MONDAY	TUESDAY
	WEEK 5		1
	6 WEEK 6	7	8
	13 WEEK 7	14	15
	20 WEEK 8	21	22
	27 WEEK 9	28	

	SU	MO	TU	WE	TH	FR	SA
JANUARY							
W52							1
W1	2	3	4	5	6	7	8
W2	9	10	11	12	13	14	15
W3	16	17	18	19	20	21	22
W4	23	24	25	26	27	28	29
W5	30	31					

	SU	MO	TU	WE	TH	FR	SA
MARCH							
W9			1	2	3	4	5
W10	6	7	8	9	10	11	12
W11	13	14	15	16	17	18	19
W12	20	21	22	23	24	25	26
W13	27	28	29	30	31		

WEDNESDAY	THURSDAY	FRIDAY	SATURDAY
2	3	4	5
9	10	11	12
16	17	18	19
23	24	25	26

FEBRUARY
OVERVIEW

FOCUS:

REMINDERS

THINGS TO REMEMBER

- ☐
- ☐
- ☐
- ☐
- ☐
- ☐
- ☐
- ☐
- ☐
- ☐
- ☐
- ☐

GOAL

GOAL

GOAL

GOAL

Master To Do List

- [ ]
- [ ] Due Date
- [ ] Due Date
- [ ] Due Date
- [ ] Due Date
- [ ] Due Date
- [ ] Due Date
- [ ] Due Date
- [ ] Due Date
- [ ] Due Date
- [ ] Due Date
- [ ] Due Date
- [ ] Due Date
- [ ] Due Date
- [ ] Due Date
- [ ] Due Date
- [ ] Due Date
- [ ] Due Date
- [ ] Due Date
- [ ] Due Date
- [ ] Due Date
- [ ] Due Date
- [ ] Due Date
- [ ] Due Date
- [ ] Due Date

WORD COUNT TRACKER

GOAL FOR THIS MONTH	I ACHIEVED

YEAR TO DATE: _____

FOCUS THIS WEEK:

WEEK 5   JANUARY 30 – FEBRUARY 5

TOP PRIORITIES   APPOINTMENTS / DEADLINES

/
/
/
/
/
/

WRITING:

MARKETING   NOTES

LIST SOMETHING GOOD FROM THIS WEEK.   LIST HOW YOU CAN MAKE NEXT WEEK BETTER.

	SU	MO	TU	WE	TH	FR	SA
W5	30	31	1	2	3	4	5
W6	6	7	8	9	10	11	12
W7	13	14	15	16	17	18	19
W8	20	21	22	23	24	25	26
W9	27	28					

FEBRUARY

SUNDAY | 30

MONDAY | 31

TUESDAY | 01

WEDNESDAY | 02

THURSDAY | 03

FRIDAY | 04

SATURDAY | 05

REMEMBER FOR NEXT WEEK

WRITING THIS WEEK

WEEK 5   JANUARY 30 – FEBRUARY 5

What I'm writing this week? And how will I measure it (words, scenes, etc)?

When will I get it done?

What do I need to make it happen?

What could keep me from reaching my goal?

How'd I do? Did I reach my goal? Exceed my goal? Miss my goal?

What can I change next week to improve my outcome?

Do I need assistance to make it happen? If so, who?

FOCUS THIS WEEK:

WEEK 6 FEBRUARY 6 – FEBRUARY 12

TOP PRIORITIES **APPOINTMENTS / DEADLINES**

/
/
/
/
/
/

WRITING:

MARKETING **NOTES**

LIST SOMETHING GOOD FROM THIS WEEK. LIST HOW YOU CAN MAKE NEXT WEEK BETTER.

	SU	MO	TU	WE	TH	FR	SA
W5				1	2	3	4	5
W6	6	7	8	9	10	11	12
W7	13	14	15	16	17	18	19
W8	20	21	22	23	24	25	26
W9	27	28					

FEBRUARY

SUNDAY | 06

MONDAY | 07

TUESDAY | 08

WEDNESDAY | 09

THURSDAY | 10

FRIDAY | 11

SATURDAY | 12

REMEMBER FOR NEXT WEEK

WRITING THIS WEEK

WEEK 6   FEBRUARY 6 – FEBRUARY 12

What I'm writing this week? And how will I measure it (words, scenes, etc)?

When will I get it done?

What do I need to make it happen?

What could keep me from reaching my goal?

How'd I do? Did I reach my goal? Exceed my goal? Miss my goal?

What can I change next week to improve my outcome?

Do I need assistance to make it happen? If so, who?

FOCUS THIS WEEK:

WEEK 7 FEBRUARY 13 – FEBRUARY 19

TOP PRIORITIES   APPOINTMENTS / DEADLINES

_____   _____ / _____
_____   _____ / _____
_____   _____ / _____
_____   _____ / _____
_____   _____ / _____
_____   _____ / _____

WRITING:

_____
_____
_____
_____
_____
_____
_____
_____

MARKETING   NOTES

_____   _____
_____   _____
_____   _____
_____   _____
_____   _____
_____   _____

LIST SOMETHING GOOD FROM THIS WEEK.   LIST HOW YOU CAN MAKE NEXT WEEK BETTER.

	SU	MO	TU	WE	TH	FR	SA
W5			1	2	3	4	5
W6	6	7	8	9	10	11	12
W7	13	14	15	16	17	18	19
W8	20	21	22	23	24	25	26
W9	27	28					

FEBRUARY

SUNDAY | 13

MONDAY | 14

TUESDAY | 15

WEDNESDAY | 16

THURSDAY | 17

FRIDAY | 18

SATURDAY | 19

REMEMBER FOR NEXT WEEK

WRITING THIS WEEK

WEEK 7   FEBRUARY 13 – FEBRUARY 19

What I'm writing this week? And how will I measure it (words, scenes, etc)?

When will I get it done?

What do I need to make it happen?

What could keep me from reaching my goal?

How'd I do? Did I reach my goal? Exceed my goal? Miss my goal?

What can I change next week to improve my outcome?

Do I need assistance to make it happen? If so, who?

FOCUS THIS WEEK:

WEEK 8   FEBRUARY 20 – FEBRUARY 26

TOP PRIORITIES	APPOINTMENTS / DEADLINES
_____	_____ / _____
_____	_____ / _____
_____	_____ / _____
_____	_____ / _____
_____	_____ / _____
_____	_____ / _____

WRITING:

_____
_____
_____
_____
_____
_____
_____
_____

MARKETING	NOTES
_____	_____
_____	_____
_____	_____
_____	_____
_____	_____

LIST SOMETHING GOOD FROM THIS WEEK.   LIST HOW YOU CAN MAKE NEXT WEEK BETTER.

	SU	MO	TU	WE	TH	FR	SA
W5			1	2	3	4	5
W6	6	7	8	9	10	11	12
W7	13	14	15	16	17	18	19
W8	20	21	22	23	24	25	26
W9	27	28					

FEBRUARY

SUNDAY | 20

MONDAY | 21

TUESDAY | 22

WEDNESDAY | 23

THURSDAY | 24

FRIDAY | 25

SATURDAY | 26

REMEMBER FOR NEXT WEEK

WRITING THIS WEEK

WEEK 8   FEBRUARY 20 – FEBRUARY 26

What I'm writing this week? And how will I measure it (words, scenes, etc)?

When will I get it done?

What do I need to make it happen?

What could keep me from reaching my goal?

How'd I do? Did I reach my goal? Exceed my goal? Miss my goal?

What can I change next week to improve my outcome?

Do I need assistance to make it happen? If so, who?

FEBRUARY
REVIEW

MY GOALS FOR THIS MONTH:

THIS MONTH I ACHIEVED:

WHAT WORKED:

WHAT DIDN'T WORK:

DO MORE OF:

DO LESS OF:

INCOME TRACKER

GOAL FOR THIS MONTH	I ACHIEVED

Date	Source	Description	Amount
		TOTAL INCOME	

EXPENSE TRACKER

GOAL FOR THIS MONTH	I ACHIEVED

Date	Category	Description	Amount
	TOTAL EXPENSES		

...my story matters.

MARCH 2022

MARCH
2022

FOCUS:

NOTES	SUNDAY	MONDAY	TUESDAY
	WEEK 9		1
	6 WEEK 10	7	8
	13 WEEK 11	14	15
	20 WEEK 12	21	22
	27 WEEK 13	28	29

FEBRUARY

	SU	MO	TU	WE	TH	FR	SA
W5			1	2	3	4	5
W6	6	7	8	9	10	11	12
W7	13	14	15	16	17	18	19
W8	20	21	22	23	24	25	26
W9	27	28					

APRIL

	SU	MO	TU	WE	TH	FR	SA
W13						1	2
W14	3	4	5	6	7	8	9
W15	10	11	12	13	14	15	16
W16	17	18	19	20	21	22	23
W17	24	25	26	27	28	29	30

WEDNESDAY	THURSDAY	FRIDAY	SATURDAY
2	3	4	5
9	10	11	12
16	17	18	19
23	24	25	26
30	31		

MARCH
OVERVIEW

FOCUS:

REMINDERS

GOAL

GOAL

GOAL

THINGS TO REMEMBER

GOAL

GOAL

- ☐
- ☐
- ☐
- ☐
- ☐
- ☐
- ☐
- ☐
- ☐
- ☐
- ☐
- ☐

Master To Do List

- [ ]
- [ ] _____ Due Date
- [ ] _____ Due Date
- [ ] _____ Due Date
- [ ] _____ Due Date
- [ ] _____ Due Date
- [ ] _____ Due Date
- [ ] _____ Due Date
- [ ] _____ Due Date
- [ ] _____ Due Date
- [ ] _____ Due Date
- [ ] _____ Due Date
- [ ] _____ Due Date
- [ ] _____ Due Date
- [ ] _____ Due Date
- [ ] _____ Due Date
- [ ] _____ Due Date
- [ ] _____ Due Date
- [ ] _____ Due Date
- [ ] _____ Due Date
- [ ] _____ Due Date
- [ ] _____ Due Date
- [ ] _____ Due Date
- [ ] _____ Due Date
- [ ] _____ Due Date

WORD COUNT TRACKER

GOAL FOR THIS MONTH	I ACHIEVED

YEAR TO DATE: _____

FOCUS THIS WEEK:

WEEK 9   FEBRUARY 27 – MARCH 5

TOP PRIORITIES	APPOINTMENTS / DEADLINES

WRITING:

MARKETING	NOTES

LIST SOMETHING GOOD FROM THIS WEEK.   LIST HOW YOU CAN MAKE NEXT WEEK BETTER.

	SU	MO	TU	WE	TH	FR	SA
W9	27	28	1	2	3	4	5
W10	6	7	8	9	10	11	12
W11	13	14	15	16	17	18	19
W12	20	21	22	23	24	25	26
W13	27	28	29	30	31		

MARCH

SUNDAY | 27

MONDAY | 28

TUESDAY | 01

WEDNESDAY | 02

THURSDAY | 03

FRIDAY | 04

SATURDAY | 05

REMEMBER FOR NEXT WEEK

WRITING THIS WEEK

WEEK 9   FEBRUARY 27 – MARCH 5

What I'm writing this week? And how will I measure it (words, scenes, etc)?

When will I get it done?

What do I need to make it happen?

What could keep me from reaching my goal?

How'd I do? Did I reach my goal? Exceed my goal? Miss my goal?

What can I change next week to improve my outcome?

Do I need assistance to make it happen? If so, who?

FOCUS THIS WEEK:

WEEK 10 — MARCH 6 – MARCH 12

TOP PRIORITIES

APPOINTMENTS / DEADLINES

/
/
/
/
/
/

WRITING:

MARKETING

NOTES

LIST SOMETHING GOOD FROM THIS WEEK.

LIST HOW YOU CAN MAKE NEXT WEEK BETTER.

	SU	MO	TU	WE	TH	FR	SA
W9			1	2	3	4	5
W10	6	7	8	9	10	11	12
W11	13	14	15	16	17	18	19
W12	20	21	22	23	24	25	26
W13	27	28	29	30	31		

MARCH

SUNDAY | 06

MONDAY | 07

TUESDAY | 08

WEDNESDAY | 09

THURSDAY | 10

FRIDAY | 11

SATURDAY | 12

REMEMBER FOR NEXT WEEK

WRITING THIS WEEK

WEEK 10 MARCH 6 – MARCH 12

What I'm writing this week? And how will I measure it (words, scenes, etc)?

When will I get it done?

What do I need to make it happen?

What could keep me from reaching my goal?

How'd I do? Did I reach my goal? Exceed my goal? Miss my goal?

What can I change next week to improve my outcome?

Do I need assistance to make it happen? If so, who?

FOCUS THIS WEEK:

WEEK 11 — MARCH 13 – MARCH 19

TOP PRIORITIES

APPOINTMENTS / DEADLINES

/
/
/
/
/
/

WRITING:

MARKETING

NOTES

LIST SOMETHING GOOD FROM THIS WEEK.

LIST HOW YOU CAN MAKE NEXT WEEK BETTER.

	SU	MO	TU	WE	TH	FR	SA
W9			1	2	3	4	5
W10	6	7	8	9	10	11	12
W11	13	14	15	16	17	18	19
W12	20	21	22	23	24	25	26
W13	27	28	29	30	31		

MARCH

SUNDAY | 13

MONDAY | 14

TUESDAY | 15

WEDNESDAY | 16

THURSDAY | 17

FRIDAY | 18

SATURDAY | 19

REMEMBER FOR NEXT WEEK

WRITING THIS WEEK

WEEK 11   MARCH 13 – MARCH 19

What I'm writing this week? And how will I measure it (words, scenes, etc)?

When will I get it done?

What do I need to make it happen?

What could keep me from reaching my goal?

How'd I do? Did I reach my goal? Exceed my goal? Miss my goal?

What can I change next week to improve my outcome?

Do I need assistance to make it happen? If so, who?

FOCUS THIS WEEK:

WEEK 12   MARCH 20 – MARCH 26

TOP PRIORITIES   APPOINTMENTS / DEADLINES

WRITING:

MARKETING   NOTES

LIST SOMETHING GOOD FROM THIS WEEK.   LIST HOW YOU CAN MAKE NEXT WEEK BETTER.

	SU	MO	TU	WE	TH	FR	SA
W9			1	2	3	4	5
W10	6	7	8	9	10	11	12
W11	13	14	15	16	17	18	19
W12	20	21	22	23	24	25	26
W13	27	28	29	30	31		

MARCH

SUNDAY | 20

MONDAY | 21

TUESDAY | 22

WEDNESDAY | 23

THURSDAY | 24

FRIDAY | 25

SATURDAY | 26

REMEMBER FOR NEXT WEEK

WRITING THIS WEEK

WEEK 12　　　　　　　　　　　　　　　　　　　　　　　　　　　　MARCH 20 - MARCH 26

What I'm writing this week? And how will I measure it (words, scenes, etc)?

When will I get it done?

What do I need to make it happen?

What could keep me from reaching my goal?

How'd I do? Did I reach my goal? Exceed my goal? Miss my goal?

What can I change next week to improve my outcome?

Do I need assistance to make it happen? If so, who?

FOCUS THIS WEEK:

WEEK 13 MARCH 27 - APRIL 2

TOP PRIORITIES APPOINTMENTS / DEADLINES

/
/
/
/
/
/

WRITING:

MARKETING NOTES

LIST SOMETHING GOOD FROM THIS WEEK. LIST HOW YOU CAN MAKE NEXT WEEK BETTER.

	SU	MO	TU	WE	TH	FR	SA
W9				1	2	3	4	5
W10	6	7	8	9	10	11	12
W11	13	14	15	16	17	18	19
W12	20	21	22	23	24	25	26
W13	27	28	29	30	31	1	2

MARCH

SUNDAY | 27

MONDAY | 28

TUESDAY | 29

WEDNESDAY | 30

THURSDAY | 31

FRIDAY | 01

SATURDAY | 02

REMEMBER FOR NEXT WEEK

WRITING THIS WEEK

WEEK 13   MARCH 27 – APRIL 2

What I'm writing this week? And how will I measure it (words, scenes, etc)?

When will I get it done?

What do I need to make it happen?

What could keep me from reaching my goal?

How'd I do? Did I reach my goal? Exceed my goal? Miss my goal?

What can I change next week to improve my outcome?

Do I need assistance to make it happen? If so, who?

MARCH
REVIEW

MY GOALS FOR THIS MONTH:
_____
_____
_____
_____
_____
_____

THIS MONTH I ACHIEVED:
_____
_____
_____
_____

WHAT WORKED:
_____
_____
_____
_____

WHAT DIDN'T WORK:
_____
_____
_____
_____

DO MORE OF: DO LESS OF:
_____   _____
_____   _____
_____   _____
_____   _____

INCOME TRACKER

GOAL FOR THIS MONTH	I ACHIEVED

Date	Source	Description	Amount
		TOTAL INCOME	

EXPENSE TRACKER

GOAL FOR THIS MONTH	I ACHIEVED

Date	Category	Description	Amount
	TOTAL EXPENSES		

...my story matters.

APRIL 2022

APRIL
2022

FOCUS:

NOTES	SUNDAY	MONDAY	TUESDAY
	WEEK 13		
	3 WEEK 14	4	5
	10 WEEK 15	11	12
	17 WEEK 16	18	19
	24 WEEK 17	25	26

	SU	MO	TU	WE	TH	FR	SA
W9			1	2	3	4	5
W10	6	7	8	9	10	11	12
W11	13	14	15	16	17	18	19
W12	20	21	22	23	24	25	26
W13	27	28	29	30	31		

MARCH

	SU	MO	TU	WE	TH	FR	SA
W18	1	2	3	4	5	6	7
W19	8	9	10	11	12	13	14
W20	15	16	17	18	19	20	21
W21	22	23	24	25	26	27	28
W22	29	30	31				

MAY

WEDNESDAY	THURSDAY	FRIDAY	SATURDAY
		1	2
6	7	8	9
13	14	15	16
20	21	22	23
27	28	29	30

APRIL
OVERVIEW

FOCUS:

REMINDERS

GOAL

GOAL

GOAL

THINGS TO REMEMBER

GOAL

Master To Do List

- [ ]
- [ ] _____ Due Date _____
- [ ] _____ Due Date _____
- [ ] _____ Due Date _____
- [ ] _____ Due Date _____
- [ ] _____ Due Date _____
- [ ] _____ Due Date _____
- [ ] _____ Due Date _____
- [ ] _____ Due Date _____
- [ ] _____ Due Date _____
- [ ] _____ Due Date _____
- [ ] _____ Due Date _____
- [ ] _____ Due Date _____
- [ ] _____ Due Date _____
- [ ] _____ Due Date _____
- [ ] _____ Due Date _____
- [ ] _____ Due Date _____
- [ ] _____ Due Date _____
- [ ] _____ Due Date _____
- [ ] _____ Due Date _____
- [ ] _____ Due Date _____
- [ ] _____ Due Date _____
- [ ] _____ Due Date _____
- [ ] _____ Due Date _____
- [ ] _____ Due Date _____

WORD COUNT TRACKER

GOAL FOR THIS MONTH	I ACHIEVED

YEAR TO DATE: _____

FOCUS THIS WEEK:

WEEK 14   APRIL 3 – APRIL 9

TOP PRIORITIES   APPOINTMENTS / DEADLINES

_____   _____ / _____
_____   _____ / _____
_____   _____ / _____
_____   _____ / _____
_____   _____ / _____
_____   _____ / _____

WRITING:

_____
_____
_____
_____
_____
_____
_____
_____
_____

MARKETING   NOTES

_____   _____
_____   _____
_____   _____
_____   _____
_____   _____

LIST SOMETHING GOOD FROM THIS WEEK.   LIST HOW YOU CAN MAKE NEXT WEEK BETTER.

	SU	MO	TU	WE	TH	FR	SA
W13						1	2
W14	3	4	5	6	7	8	9
W15	10	11	12	13	14	15	16
W16	17	18	19	20	21	22	23
W17	24	25	26	27	28	29	30

APRIL

SUNDAY | 03

MONDAY | 04

TUESDAY | 05

WEDNESDAY | 06

THURSDAY | 07

FRIDAY | 08

SATURDAY | 09

REMEMBER FOR NEXT WEEK

WRITING THIS WEEK

WEEK 14   APRIL 3 – APRIL 9

What I'm writing this week? And how will I measure it (words, scenes, etc)?

When will I get it done?

What do I need to make it happen?

What could keep me from reaching my goal?

How'd I do? Did I reach my goal? Exceed my goal? Miss my goal?

What can I change next week to improve my outcome?

Do I need assistance to make it happen? If so, who?

FOCUS THIS WEEK:

WEEK 15   APRIL 10 – APRIL 16

TOP PRIORITIES	APPOINTMENTS / DEADLINES
_____	_____ / _____
_____	_____ / _____
_____	_____ / _____
_____	_____ / _____
_____	_____ / _____
_____	_____ / _____

WRITING:

_____
_____
_____
_____
_____
_____
_____
_____

MARKETING	NOTES
_____	_____
_____	_____
_____	_____
_____	_____
_____	_____
_____	_____

LIST SOMETHING GOOD FROM THIS WEEK.   LIST HOW YOU CAN MAKE NEXT WEEK BETTER.

	SU	MO	TU	WE	TH	FR	SA
W13						1	2
W14	3	4	5	6	7	8	9
W15	10	11	12	13	14	15	16
W16	17	18	19	20	21	22	23
W17	24	25	26	27	28	29	30

APRIL

SUNDAY | 10

MONDAY | 11

TUESDAY | 12

WEDNESDAY | 13

THURSDAY | 14

FRIDAY | 15

SATURDAY | 16

REMEMBER FOR NEXT WEEK

WRITING THIS WEEK

WEEK 15 APRIL 10 – APRIL 16

What I'm writing this week? And how will I measure it (words, scenes, etc)?

When will I get it done?

What do I need to make it happen?

What could keep me from reaching my goal?

How'd I do? Did I reach my goal? Exceed my goal? Miss my goal?

What can I change next week to improve my outcome?

Do I need assistance to make it happen? If so, who?

FOCUS THIS WEEK:

WEEK 16　　　　　　　　　　　　　　　　　　　　　　　　　　　　　　APRIL 17 – APRIL 23

TOP PRIORITIES　　　　　　　　APPOINTMENTS / DEADLINES

/
/
/
/
/
/

WRITING:

MARKETING　　　　　　　　　　　　**NOTES**

LIST SOMETHING GOOD FROM THIS WEEK.　　　　LIST HOW YOU CAN MAKE NEXT WEEK BETTER.

	SU	MO	TU	WE	TH	FR	SA
W13						1	2
W14	3	4	5	6	7	8	9
W15	10	11	12	13	14	15	16
W16	17	18	19	20	21	22	23
W17	24	25	26	27	28	29	30

APRIL

SUNDAY | 17

MONDAY | 18

TUESDAY | 19

WEDNESDAY | 20

THURSDAY | 21

FRIDAY | 22

SATURDAY | 23

REMEMBER FOR NEXT WEEK

WRITING THIS WEEK

WEEK 16 APRIL 17 – APRIL 23

What I'm writing this week? And how will I measure it (words, scenes, etc)?

When will I get it done?

What do I need to make it happen?

What could keep me from reaching my goal?

How'd I do? Did I reach my goal? Exceed my goal? Miss my goal?

What can I change next week to improve my outcome?

Do I need assistance to make it happen? If so, who?

FOCUS THIS WEEK:

WEEK 17 APRIL 24 – APRIL 30

TOP PRIORITIES APPOINTMENTS / DEADLINES

/
/
/
/
/
/

WRITING:

MARKETING **NOTES**

LIST SOMETHING GOOD FROM THIS WEEK. LIST HOW YOU CAN MAKE NEXT WEEK BETTER.

	SU	MO	TU	WE	TH	FR	SA
W13						1	2
W14	3	4	5	6	7	8	9
APRIL W15	10	11	12	13	14	15	16
W16	17	18	19	20	21	22	23
W17	24	25	26	27	28	29	30

SUNDAY | 24

MONDAY | 25

TUESDAY | 26

WEDNESDAY | 27

THURSDAY | 28

FRIDAY | 29

SATURDAY | 30

REMEMBER FOR NEXT WEEK

WRITING THIS WEEK

WEEK 17   APRIL 24 – APRIL 30

What I'm writing this week? And how will I measure it (words, scenes, etc)?

When will I get it done?

What do I need to make it happen?

What could keep me from reaching my goal?

How'd I do? Did I reach my goal? Exceed my goal? Miss my goal?

What can I change next week to improve my outcome?

Do I need assistance to make it happen? If so, who?

APRIL
REVIEW

MY GOALS FOR THIS MONTH:
_____
_____
_____
_____
_____
_____

THIS MONTH I ACHIEVED:
_____
_____
_____
_____
_____

WHAT WORKED:
_____
_____
_____
_____
_____

WHAT DIDN'T WORK:
_____
_____
_____
_____

DO MORE OF: DO LESS OF:
_____   _____
_____   _____
_____   _____
_____   _____
_____   _____

INCOME TRACKER

GOAL FOR THIS MONTH	I ACHIEVED

Date	Source	Description	Amount
		TOTAL INCOME	

EXPENSE TRACKER

GOAL FOR THIS MONTH	I ACHIEVED

Date	Category	Description	Amount
	TOTAL EXPENSES		

...my story matters.

MAY 2022

MAY
2022

FOCUS:

NOTES	SUNDAY	MONDAY	TUESDAY
	1 WEEK 18	2	3
	8 WEEK 19	9	10
	15 WEEK 20	16	17
	22 WEEK 21	23	24
	29 WEEK 22	30	31

	SU MO TU WE TH FR SA		SU MO TU WE TH FR SA
	W13 1 2		W22 1 2 3 4
APRIL	W14 3 4 5 6 7 8 9	JUNE	W23 5 6 7 8 9 10 11
	W15 10 11 12 13 14 15 16		W24 12 13 14 15 16 17 18
	W16 17 18 19 20 21 22 23		W25 19 20 21 22 23 24 25
	W17 24 25 26 27 28 29 30		W26 26 27 28 29 30

WEDNESDAY	THURSDAY	FRIDAY	SATURDAY
4	5	6	7
11	12	13	14
18	19	20	21
25	26	27	28

MAY
OVERVIEW

FOCUS:

REMINDERS

THINGS TO REMEMBER

- [ ]
- [ ]
- [ ]
- [ ]
- [ ]
- [ ]
- [ ]
- [ ]
- [ ]
- [ ]
- [ ]
- [ ]

GOAL

GOAL

GOAL

GOAL

Master To Do List

- [ ]
- [ ] _____ Due Date
- [ ] _____ Due Date
- [ ] _____ Due Date
- [ ] _____ Due Date
- [ ] _____ Due Date
- [ ] _____ Due Date
- [ ] _____ Due Date
- [ ] _____ Due Date
- [ ] _____ Due Date
- [ ] _____ Due Date
- [ ] _____ Due Date
- [ ] _____ Due Date
- [ ] _____ Due Date
- [ ] _____ Due Date
- [ ] _____ Due Date
- [ ] _____ Due Date
- [ ] _____ Due Date
- [ ] _____ Due Date
- [ ] _____ Due Date
- [ ] _____ Due Date
- [ ] _____ Due Date
- [ ] _____ Due Date
- [ ] _____ Due Date

WORD COUNT TRACKER

GOAL FOR THIS MONTH	I ACHIEVED

YEAR TO DATE: _____

FOCUS THIS WEEK:

WEEK 18   MAY 1 – MAY 7

TOP PRIORITIES	APPOINTMENTS / DEADLINES
	/
	/
	/
	/
	/
	/

WRITING:

MARKETING   **NOTES**

LIST SOMETHING GOOD FROM THIS WEEK.   LIST HOW YOU CAN MAKE NEXT WEEK BETTER.

	SU	MO	TU	WE	TH	FR	SA
W18	1	2	3	4	5	6	7
W19	8	9	10	11	12	13	14
W20	15	16	17	18	19	20	21
W21	22	23	24	25	26	27	28
W22	29	30	31				

MAY

SUNDAY | 01

MONDAY | 02

TUESDAY | 03

WEDNESDAY | 04

THURSDAY | 05

FRIDAY | 06

SATURDAY | 07

REMEMBER FOR NEXT WEEK

WRITING THIS WEEK

WEEK 18 — MAY 1 – MAY 7

What I'm writing this week? And how will I measure it (words, scenes, etc)?

When will I get it done?

What do I need to make it happen?

What could keep me from reaching my goal?

How'd I do? Did I reach my goal? Exceed my goal? Miss my goal?

What can I change next week to improve my outcome?

Do I need assistance to make it happen? If so, who?

FOCUS THIS WEEK:

WEEK 19   MAY 8 – MAY 14

TOP PRIORITIES	APPOINTMENTS / DEADLINES
	/
	/
	/
	/
	/
	/

WRITING:

MARKETING	NOTES

LIST SOMETHING GOOD FROM THIS WEEK.   LIST HOW YOU CAN MAKE NEXT WEEK BETTER.

	SU	MO	TU	WE	TH	FR	SA
W18	1	2	3	4	5	6	7
W19	8	9	10	11	12	13	14
W20	15	16	17	18	19	20	21
W21	22	23	24	25	26	27	28
W22	29	30	31				

MAY

SUNDAY | 08

MONDAY | 09

TUESDAY | 10

WEDNESDAY | 11

THURSDAY | 12

FRIDAY | 13

SATURDAY | 14

REMEMBER FOR NEXT WEEK

WRITING THIS WEEK

WEEK 19   MAY 8 – MAY 14

What I'm writing this week? And how will I measure it (words, scenes, etc)?

When will I get it done?

What do I need to make it happen?

What could keep me from reaching my goal?

How'd I do? Did I reach my goal? Exceed my goal? Miss my goal?

What can I change next week to improve my outcome?

Do I need assistance to make it happen? If so, who?

FOCUS THIS WEEK:

WEEK 20   MAY 15 – MAY 21

TOP PRIORITIES	APPOINTMENTS / DEADLINES
_____	_____ / _____
_____	_____ / _____
_____	_____ / _____
_____	_____ / _____
_____	_____ / _____
_____	_____ / _____

WRITING:

_____
_____
_____
_____
_____
_____
_____
_____

MARKETING	NOTES
_____	_____
_____	_____
_____	_____
_____	_____
_____	_____
_____	_____

LIST SOMETHING GOOD FROM THIS WEEK.   LIST HOW YOU CAN MAKE NEXT WEEK BETTER.

	SU	MO	TU	WE	TH	FR	SA
W18	1	2	3	4	5	6	7
W19	8	9	10	11	12	13	14
W20	15	16	17	18	19	20	21
W21	22	23	24	25	26	27	28
W22	29	30	31				

MAY

SUNDAY | 15

MONDAY | 16

TUESDAY | 17

WEDNESDAY | 18

THURSDAY | 19

FRIDAY | 20

SATURDAY | 21

REMEMBER FOR NEXT WEEK

WRITING THIS WEEK

WEEK 20   MAY 15 – MAY 21

What I'm writing this week? And how will I measure it (words, scenes, etc)?

When will I get it done?

What do I need to make it happen?

What could keep me from reaching my goal?

How'd I do? Did I reach my goal? Exceed my goal? Miss my goal?

What can I change next week to improve my outcome?

Do I need assistance to make it happen? If so, who?

FOCUS THIS WEEK:

WEEK 21   MAY 22 - MAY 28

TOP PRIORITIES	APPOINTMENTS / DEADLINES
_____	____ / _____
_____	____ / _____
_____	____ / _____
_____	____ / _____
_____	____ / _____
_____	____ / _____

WRITING:

_____
_____
_____
_____
_____
_____
_____
_____

MARKETING	NOTES
_____	_____
_____	_____
_____	_____
_____	_____
_____	_____
_____	_____

LIST SOMETHING GOOD FROM THIS WEEK.   LIST HOW YOU CAN MAKE NEXT WEEK BETTER.

	SU	MO	TU	WE	TH	FR	SA
W18	1	2	3	4	5	6	7
W19	8	9	10	11	12	13	14
W20	15	16	17	18	19	20	21
W21	22	23	24	25	26	27	28
W22	29	30	31				

MAY

SUNDAY | 22

MONDAY | 23

TUESDAY | 24

WEDNESDAY | 25

THURSDAY | 26

FRIDAY | 27

SATURDAY | 28

REMEMBER FOR NEXT WEEK

WRITING THIS WEEK

WEEK 21 — MAY 22 - MAY 28

What I'm writing this week? And how will I measure it (words, scenes, etc)?

When will I get it done?

What do I need to make it happen?

What could keep me from reaching my goal?

How'd I do? Did I reach my goal? Exceed my goal? Miss my goal?

What can I change next week to improve my outcome?

Do I need assistance to make it happen? If so, who?

MAY
REVIEW

MY GOALS FOR THIS MONTH:

THIS MONTH I ACHIEVED:

WHAT WORKED:

WHAT DIDN'T WORK:

DO MORE OF:

DO LESS OF:

INCOME TRACKER

GOAL FOR THIS MONTH	I ACHIEVED

Date	Source	Description	Amount
		TOTAL INCOME	

EXPENSE TRACKER

GOAL FOR THIS MONTH	I ACHIEVED

Date	Category	Description	Amount
	TOTAL EXPENSES		

...my story matters.

JUNE 2022

JUNE
2022

FOCUS:

NOTES	SUNDAY	MONDAY	TUESDAY
	WEEK 22		
	5 WEEK 23	6	7
	12 WEEK 24	13	14
	19 WEEK 25	20	21
	26 WEEK 26	27	28

MAY

	SU	MO	TU	WE	TH	FR	SA
W18		1	2	3	4	5	6	7
W19	8	9	10	11	12	13	14
W20	15	16	17	18	19	20	21
W21	22	23	24	25	26	27	28
W22	29	30	31				

JULY

	SU	MO	TU	WE	TH	FR	SA
W26						1	2
W27	3	4	5	6	7	8	9
W28	10	11	12	13	14	15	16
W29	17	18	19	20	21	22	23
W30	24	25	26	27	28	29	30
W31	31						

WEDNESDAY	THURSDAY	FRIDAY	SATURDAY
1	2	3	4
8	9	10	11
15	16	17	18
22	23	24	25
29	30		

JUNE
OVERVIEW

FOCUS:

REMINDERS

GOAL

GOAL

GOAL

THINGS TO REMEMBER

- [ ]
- [ ]
- [ ]
- [ ]
- [ ]
- [ ]
- [ ]
- [ ]
- [ ]
- [ ]
- [ ]
- [ ]

GOAL

Master To Do List

- [ ]
- [ ] _____ Due Date
- [ ] _____ Due Date
- [ ] _____ Due Date
- [ ] _____ Due Date
- [ ] _____ Due Date
- [ ] _____ Due Date
- [ ] _____ Due Date
- [ ] _____ Due Date
- [ ] _____ Due Date
- [ ] _____ Due Date
- [ ] _____ Due Date
- [ ] _____ Due Date
- [ ] _____ Due Date
- [ ] _____ Due Date
- [ ] _____ Due Date
- [ ] _____ Due Date
- [ ] _____ Due Date
- [ ] _____ Due Date
- [ ] _____ Due Date
- [ ] _____ Due Date
- [ ] _____ Due Date
- [ ] _____ Due Date
- [ ] _____ Due Date

WORD COUNT TRACKER

GOAL FOR THIS MONTH	I ACHIEVED

YEAR TO DATE:

FOCUS THIS WEEK:

WEEK 22　　　　　　　　　　　　　　　　　　　　　　　　　　　　　　　MAY 29 – JUNE 4

　　　　　　　TOP PRIORITIES　　　　　　　　　APPOINTMENTS / DEADLINES

　　　　　　　　　　　　　　　　　　　　　　　　　　　/
　　　　　　　　　　　　　　　　　　　　　　　　　　　/
　　　　　　　　　　　　　　　　　　　　　　　　　　　/
　　　　　　　　　　　　　　　　　　　　　　　　　　　/
　　　　　　　　　　　　　　　　　　　　　　　　　　　/
　　　　　　　　　　　　　　　　　　　　　　　　　　　/

WRITING:

　　　　　　　　　MARKETING　　　　　　　　　　　　　　NOTES

LIST SOMETHING GOOD FROM THIS WEEK.　　　LIST HOW YOU CAN MAKE NEXT WEEK BETTER.

	SU	MO	TU	WE	TH	FR	SA
W22	29	30	31	1	2	3	4
W23	5	6	7	8	9	10	11
W24	12	13	14	15	16	17	18
W25	19	20	21	22	23	24	25
W26	26	27	28	29	30		

JUNE

SUNDAY | 29

MONDAY | 30

TUESDAY | 31

WEDNESDAY | 01

THURSDAY | 02

FRIDAY | 03

SATURDAY | 04

REMEMBER FOR NEXT WEEK

WRITING THIS WEEK

WEEK 22   MAY 29 – JUNE 4

What I'm writing this week? And how will I measure it (words, scenes, etc)?

When will I get it done?

What do I need to make it happen?

What could keep me from reaching my goal?

How'd I do? Did I reach my goal? Exceed my goal? Miss my goal?

What can I change next week to improve my outcome?

Do I need assistance to make it happen? If so, who?

FOCUS THIS WEEK:

WEEK 23 JUNE 5 – JUNE 11

TOP PRIORITIES

APPOINTMENTS / DEADLINES

/
/
/
/
/
/

WRITING:

MARKETING

NOTES

LIST SOMETHING GOOD FROM THIS WEEK.

LIST HOW YOU CAN MAKE NEXT WEEK BETTER.

	SU	MO	TU	WE	TH	FR	SA
W22				1	2	3	4
W23	5	6	7	8	9	10	11
W24	12	13	14	15	16	17	18
W25	19	20	21	22	23	24	25
W26	26	27	28	29	30		

JUNE

SUNDAY | 05

MONDAY | 06

TUESDAY | 07

WEDNESDAY | 08

THURSDAY | 09

FRIDAY | 10

SATURDAY | 11

REMEMBER FOR NEXT WEEK

WRITING THIS WEEK

WEEK 23   JUNE 5 – JUNE 11

What I'm writing this week? And how will I measure it (words, scenes, etc)?

When will I get it done?

What do I need to make it happen?

What could keep me from reaching my goal?

How'd I do? Did I reach my goal? Exceed my goal? Miss my goal?

What can I change next week to improve my outcome?

Do I need assistance to make it happen? If so, who?

FOCUS THIS WEEK:

WEEK 24 JUNE 12 – JUNE 18

TOP PRIORITIES   APPOINTMENTS / DEADLINES

/
/
/
/
/
/

WRITING:

MARKETING   NOTES

LIST SOMETHING GOOD FROM THIS WEEK.   LIST HOW YOU CAN MAKE NEXT WEEK BETTER.

	SU	MO	TU	WE	TH	FR	SA
W22				1	2	3	4
W23	5	6	7	8	9	10	11
W24	12	13	14	15	16	17	18
W25	19	20	21	22	23	24	25
W26	26	27	28	29	30		

JUNE

SUNDAY | 12

MONDAY | 13

TUESDAY | 14

WEDNESDAY | 15

THURSDAY | 16

FRIDAY | 17

SATURDAY | 18

REMEMBER FOR NEXT WEEK

WRITING THIS WEEK

WEEK 24   JUNE 12 - JUNE 18

What I'm writing this week? And how will I measure it (words, scenes, etc)?

When will I get it done?

What do I need to make it happen?

What could keep me from reaching my goal?

How'd I do? Did I reach my goal? Exceed my goal? Miss my goal?

What can I change next week to improve my outcome?

Do I need assistance to make it happen? If so, who?

FOCUS THIS WEEK:

WEEK 25   JUNE 19 – JUNE 25

TOP PRIORITIES	APPOINTMENTS / DEADLINES

WRITING:

MARKETING	NOTES

LIST SOMETHING GOOD FROM THIS WEEK.   LIST HOW YOU CAN MAKE NEXT WEEK BETTER.

	SU	MO	TU	WE	TH	FR	SA
W22				1	2	3	4
W23	5	6	7	8	9	10	11
W24	12	13	14	15	16	17	18
W25	19	20	21	22	23	24	25
W26	26	27	28	29	30		

JUNE

SUNDAY | 19

MONDAY | 20

TUESDAY | 21

WEDNESDAY | 22

THURSDAY | 23

FRIDAY | 24

SATURDAY | 25

REMEMBER FOR NEXT WEEK

WRITING THIS WEEK

WEEK 25   JUNE 19 – JUNE 25

What I'm writing this week? And how will I measure it (words, scenes, etc)?

When will I get it done?

What do I need to make it happen?

What could keep me from reaching my goal?

How'd I do? Did I reach my goal? Exceed my goal? Miss my goal?

What can I change next week to improve my outcome?

Do I need assistance to make it happen? If so, who?

FOCUS THIS WEEK:

WEEK 26   JUNE 26 – JULY 2

TOP PRIORITIES	APPOINTMENTS / DEADLINES
_____	___ / _____
_____	___ / _____
_____	___ / _____
_____	___ / _____
_____	___ / _____
_____	___ / _____

WRITING:

MARKETING	NOTES

LIST SOMETHING GOOD FROM THIS WEEK.   LIST HOW YOU CAN MAKE NEXT WEEK BETTER.

	SU	MO	TU	WE	TH	FR	SA
W22				1	2	3	4
W23	5	6	7	8	9	10	11
W24	12	13	14	15	16	17	18
W25	19	20	21	22	23	24	25
W26	26	27	28	29	30	1	2

JUNE

SUNDAY | 26

MONDAY | 27

TUESDAY | 28

WEDNESDAY | 29

THURSDAY | 30

FRIDAY | 01

SATURDAY | 02

REMEMBER FOR NEXT WEEK

WRITING THIS WEEK

WEEK 26   JUNE 26 – JULY 2

What I'm writing this week? And how will I measure it (words, scenes, etc)?

When will I get it done?

What do I need to make it happen?

What could keep me from reaching my goal?

How'd I do? Did I reach my goal? Exceed my goal? Miss my goal?

What can I change next week to improve my outcome?

Do I need assistance to make it happen? If so, who?

JUNE
REVIEW

MY GOALS FOR THIS MONTH:
_____
_____
_____
_____
_____
_____

THIS MONTH I ACHIEVED:
_____
_____
_____
_____
_____

WHAT WORKED:
_____
_____
_____
_____
_____

WHAT DIDN'T WORK:
_____
_____
_____
_____

DO MORE OF:	DO LESS OF:
_____	_____
_____	_____
_____	_____
_____	_____
_____	_____

INCOME TRACKER

GOAL FOR THIS MONTH	I ACHIEVED

Date	Source	Description	Amount
		TOTAL INCOME	

EXPENSE TRACKER

GOAL FOR THIS MONTH	I ACHIEVED

Date	Category	Description	Amount
	TOTAL EXPENSES		

...my story matters.

JULY 2022

JULY
2022

FOCUS:

NOTES	SUNDAY	MONDAY	TUESDAY
	WEEK 26		
	3 WEEK 27	4	5
	10 WEEK 28	11	12
	17 WEEK 29	18	19
	24 WEEK 30 / 31	25	26

JUNE

	SU	MO	TU	WE	TH	FR	SA
W22				1	2	3	4
W23	5	6	7	8	9	10	11
W24	12	13	14	15	16	17	18
W25	19	20	21	22	23	24	25
W26	26	27	28	29	30		

AUGUST

	SU	MO	TU	WE	TH	FR	SA
W31		1	2	3	4	5	6
W32	7	8	9	10	11	12	13
W33	14	15	16	17	18	19	20
W34	21	22	23	24	25	26	27
W35	28	29	30	31			

WEDNESDAY	THURSDAY	FRIDAY	SATURDAY
		1	2
6	7	8	9
13	14	15	16
20	21	22	23
27	28	29	30

JULY
OVERVIEW

FOCUS:

REMINDERS

GOAL

GOAL

THINGS TO REMEMBER

- [ ]
- [ ]
- [ ]
- [ ]
- [ ]
- [ ]
- [ ]
- [ ]
- [ ]
- [ ]
- [ ]
- [ ]

GOAL

GOAL

Master To Do List

- [ ]
- [ ] Due Date
- [ ] Due Date
- [ ] Due Date
- [ ] Due Date
- [ ] Due Date
- [ ] Due Date
- [ ] Due Date
- [ ] Due Date
- [ ] Due Date
- [ ] Due Date
- [ ] Due Date
- [ ] Due Date
- [ ] Due Date
- [ ] Due Date
- [ ] Due Date
- [ ] Due Date
- [ ] Due Date
- [ ] Due Date
- [ ] Due Date
- [ ] Due Date
- [ ] Due Date
- [ ] Due Date
- [ ] Due Date
- [ ] Due Date

WORD COUNT TRACKER

GOAL FOR THIS MONTH	I ACHIEVED

YEAR TO DATE: _____

FOCUS THIS WEEK:

WEEK 27 JULY 3 – JULY 9

TOP PRIORITIES

APPOINTMENTS / DEADLINES

/
/
/
/
/
/

WRITING:

MARKETING

NOTES

LIST SOMETHING GOOD FROM THIS WEEK.

LIST HOW YOU CAN MAKE NEXT WEEK BETTER.

	SU	MO	TU	WE	TH	FR	SA
W26						1	2
W27	3	4	5	6	7	8	9
W28	10	11	12	13	14	15	16
W29	17	18	19	20	21	22	23
W30	24	25	26	27	28	29	30
W31	31						

JULY

SUNDAY | 03

MONDAY | 04

TUESDAY | 05

WEDNESDAY | 06

THURSDAY | 07

FRIDAY | 08

SATURDAY | 09

REMEMBER FOR NEXT WEEK

WRITING THIS WEEK

WEEK 27 JULY 3 – JULY 9

What I'm writing this week? And how will I measure it (words, scenes, etc)?

When will I get it done?

What do I need to make it happen?

What could keep me from reaching my goal?

How'd I do? Did I reach my goal? Exceed my goal? Miss my goal?

What can I change next week to improve my outcome?

Do I need assistance to make it happen? If so, who?

FOCUS THIS WEEK:

WEEK 28   JULY 10 – JULY 16

TOP PRIORITIES	APPOINTMENTS / DEADLINES
	/
	/
	/
	/
	/
	/

WRITING:

MARKETING

NOTES

LIST SOMETHING GOOD FROM THIS WEEK.

LIST HOW YOU CAN MAKE NEXT WEEK BETTER.

	SU	MO	TU	WE	TH	FR	SA
W26						1	2
W27	3	4	5	6	7	8	9
W28	10	11	12	13	14	15	16
W29	17	18	19	20	21	22	23
W30	24	25	26	27	28	29	30
W31	31						

JULY

SUNDAY | 10

MONDAY | 11

TUESDAY | 12

WEDNESDAY | 13

THURSDAY | 14

FRIDAY | 15

SATURDAY | 16

REMEMBER FOR NEXT WEEK

WRITING THIS WEEK

WEEK 28   JULY 10 – JULY 16

What I'm writing this week? And how will I measure it (words, scenes, etc)?

When will I get it done?

What do I need to make it happen?

What could keep me from reaching my goal?

How'd I do? Did I reach my goal? Exceed my goal? Miss my goal?

What can I change next week to improve my outcome?

Do I need assistance to make it happen? If so, who?

FOCUS THIS WEEK:

WEEK 29 JULY 17 – JULY 23

TOP PRIORITIES APPOINTMENTS / DEADLINES

/
/
/
/
/
/

WRITING:

MARKETING NOTES

LIST SOMETHING GOOD FROM THIS WEEK. LIST HOW YOU CAN MAKE NEXT WEEK BETTER.

	SU	MO	TU	WE	TH	FR	SA
W26						1	2
W27	3	4	5	6	7	8	9
W28	10	11	12	13	14	15	16
W29	17	18	19	20	21	22	23
W30	24	25	26	27	28	29	30
W31	31						

JULY

SUNDAY | 17

MONDAY | 18

TUESDAY | 19

WEDNESDAY | 20

THURSDAY | 21

FRIDAY | 22

SATURDAY | 23

REMEMBER FOR NEXT WEEK

WRITING THIS WEEK

WEEK 29　　　　　　　　　　　　　　　　　　　　　　　　　　　　　　　JULY 17 - JULY 23

What I'm writing this week? And how will I measure it (words, scenes, etc)?

When will I get it done?

What do I need to make it happen?

What could keep me from reaching my goal?

How'd I do? Did I reach my goal? Exceed my goal? Miss my goal?

What can I change next week to improve my outcome?

Do I need assistance to make it happen? If so, who?

FOCUS THIS WEEK:

WEEK 30   JULY 24 - JULY 30

TOP PRIORITIES

APPOINTMENTS / DEADLINES

/
/
/
/
/
/

WRITING:

MARKETING

NOTES

LIST SOMETHING GOOD FROM THIS WEEK.

LIST HOW YOU CAN MAKE NEXT WEEK BETTER.

	SU	MO	TU	WE	TH	FR	SA
W26	26	27	28	29	30	1	2
W27	3	4	5	6	7	8	9
W28	10	11	12	13	14	15	16
W29	17	18	19	20	21	22	23
W30	24	25	26	27	28	29	30
W31	31						

JULY

SUNDAY | 24

MONDAY | 25

TUESDAY | 26

WEDNESDAY | 27

THURSDAY | 28

FRIDAY | 29

SATURDAY | 09

REMEMBER FOR NEXT WEEK

WRITING THIS WEEK

WEEK 30   JULY 24 – JULY 30

What I'm writing this week? And how will I measure it (words, scenes, etc)?

When will I get it done?

What do I need to make it happen?

What could keep me from reaching my goal?

How'd I do? Did I reach my goal? Exceed my goal? Miss my goal?

What can I change next week to improve my outcome?

Do I need assistance to make it happen? If so, who?

JULY
REVIEW

MY GOALS FOR THIS MONTH:
_____
_____
_____
_____
_____
_____

THIS MONTH I ACHIEVED:
_____
_____
_____
_____
_____

WHAT WORKED:
_____
_____
_____
_____
_____

WHAT DIDN'T WORK:
_____
_____
_____
_____

DO MORE OF: DO LESS OF:
_____   _____
_____   _____
_____   _____
_____   _____

INCOME TRACKER

GOAL FOR THIS MONTH	I ACHIEVED

Date	Source	Description	Amount
	TOTAL INCOME		

EXPENSE TRACKER

GOAL FOR THIS MONTH	I ACHIEVED

Date	Category	Description	Amount
		TOTAL EXPENSES	

...my story matters.

AUGUST 2022

AUGUST
2022

FOCUS:

NOTES	SUNDAY	MONDAY	TUESDAY
	WEEK 31	1	2
	7 WEEK 32	8	9
	14 WEEK 33	15	16
	21 WEEK 34	22	23
	28 WEEK 35	29	30

	SU MO TU WE TH FR SA
W26	1 2
W27	3 4 5 6 7 8 9
W28	10 11 12 13 14 15 16
W29	17 18 19 20 21 22 23
W30	24 25 26 27 28 29 30
W31	31

JULY

	SU MO TU WE TH FR SA
W35	1 2 3
W36	4 5 6 7 8 9 10
W37	11 12 13 14 15 16 17
W38	18 19 20 21 22 23 24
W39	25 26 27 28 29 30

SEPTEMBER

WEDNESDAY	THURSDAY	FRIDAY	SATURDAY
3	4	5	6
10	11	12	13
17	18	19	20
24	25	26	27
31			

AUGUST
OVERVIEW

FOCUS:

REMINDERS

GOAL

GOAL

GOAL

GOAL

THINGS TO REMEMBER

- [ ]
- [ ]
- [ ]
- [ ]
- [ ]
- [ ]
- [ ]
- [ ]
- [ ]
- [ ]
- [ ]
- [ ]

Master To Do List

- [ ]
- [ ] Due Date
- [ ] Due Date
- [ ] Due Date
- [ ] Due Date
- [ ] Due Date
- [ ] Due Date
- [ ] Due Date
- [ ] Due Date
- [ ] Due Date
- [ ] Due Date
- [ ] Due Date
- [ ] Due Date
- [ ] Due Date
- [ ] Due Date
- [ ] Due Date
- [ ] Due Date
- [ ] Due Date
- [ ] Due Date
- [ ] Due Date
- [ ] Due Date
- [ ] Due Date
- [ ] Due Date
- [ ] Due Date

Due Date

WORD COUNT TRACKER

GOAL FOR THIS MONTH	I ACHIEVED

YEAR TO DATE: _____

FOCUS THIS WEEK:

WEEK 31　　　　　　　　　　　　　　　　　　　　　　　　　　　　JULY 31 – AUGUST 6

TOP PRIORITIES　　　　　　　　APPOINTMENTS / DEADLINES

/
/
/
/
/
/

WRITING:

MARKETING　　　　　　　　　　　　　　　　NOTES

LIST SOMETHING GOOD FROM THIS WEEK.　　　LIST HOW YOU CAN MAKE NEXT WEEK BETTER.

	SU	MO	TU	WE	TH	FR	SA
W31	31	1	2	3	4	5	6
W32	7	8	9	10	11	12	13
W33	14	15	16	17	18	19	20
W34	21	22	23	24	25	26	27
W35	28	29	30	31			

AUGUST

SUNDAY | 31

MONDAY | 01

TUESDAY | 02

WEDNESDAY | 03

THURSDAY | 04

FRIDAY | 05

SATURDAY | 06

REMEMBER FOR NEXT WEEK

WRITING THIS WEEK

WEEK 31 JULY 31 – AUGUST 6

What I'm writing this week? And how will I measure it (words, scenes, etc)?

When will I get it done?

What do I need to make it happen?

What could keep me from reaching my goal?

How'd I do? Did I reach my goal? Exceed my goal? Miss my goal?

What can I change next week to improve my outcome?

Do I need assistance to make it happen? If so, who?

FOCUS THIS WEEK:

WEEK 32 AUGUST 7 – AUGUST 13

TOP PRIORITIES

APPOINTMENTS / DEADLINES

/
/
/
/
/
/

WRITING:

MARKETING

NOTES

LIST SOMETHING GOOD FROM THIS WEEK.

LIST HOW YOU CAN MAKE NEXT WEEK BETTER.

	SU	MO	TU	WE	TH	FR	SA
W31		1	2	3	4	5	6
W32	7	8	9	10	11	12	13
W33	14	15	16	17	18	19	20
W34	21	22	23	24	25	26	27
W35	28	29	30	31			

AUGUST

SUNDAY | 07

MONDAY | 08

TUESDAY | 09

WEDNESDAY | 10

THURSDAY | 11

FRIDAY | 12

SATURDAY | 13

REMEMBER FOR NEXT WEEK

WRITING THIS WEEK

WEEK 32   AUGUST 7 – AUGUST 13

What I'm writing this week? And how will I measure it (words, scenes, etc)?

When will I get it done?

What do I need to make it happen?

What could keep me from reaching my goal?

How'd I do? Did I reach my goal? Exceed my goal? Miss my goal?

What can I change next week to improve my outcome?

Do I need assistance to make it happen? If so, who?

FOCUS THIS WEEK:

WEEK 33　　　　　　　　　　　　　　　　　　　　　　　　　　　　　AUGUST 14 – AUGUST 20

TOP PRIORITIES　　　　　　　**APPOINTMENTS / DEADLINES**

/
/
/
/
/
/

WRITING:

MARKETING　　　　　　　　　　　　　**NOTES**

LIST SOMETHING GOOD FROM THIS WEEK.　　　LIST HOW YOU CAN MAKE NEXT WEEK BETTER.

	SU	MO	TU	WE	TH	FR	SA
W31		1	2	3	4	5	6
W32	7	8	9	10	11	12	13
W33	14	15	16	17	18	19	20
W34	21	22	23	24	25	26	27
W35	28	29	30	31			

AUGUST

SUNDAY | 14

MONDAY | 15

TUESDAY | 16

WEDNESDAY | 17

THURSDAY | 18

FRIDAY | 19

SATURDAY | 20

REMEMBER FOR NEXT WEEK

WRITING THIS WEEK

WEEK 33	AUGUST 14 – AUGUST 20

What I'm writing this week? And how will I measure it (words, scenes, etc)?

When will I get it done?

What do I need to make it happen?

What could keep me from reaching my goal?

How'd I do? Did I reach my goal? Exceed my goal? Miss my goal?

What can I change next week to improve my outcome?

Do I need assistance to make it happen? If so, who?

FOCUS THIS WEEK:

WEEK 34 AUGUST 21 – AUGUST 27

TOP PRIORITIES | **APPOINTMENTS / DEADLINES**

/
/
/
/
/
/

WRITING:

MARKETING | **NOTES**

LIST SOMETHING GOOD FROM THIS WEEK. | LIST HOW YOU CAN MAKE NEXT WEEK BETTER.

	SU	MO	TU	WE	TH	FR	SA
W31		1	2	3	4	5	6
W32	7	8	9	10	11	12	13
W33	14	15	16	17	18	19	20
W34	21	22	23	24	25	26	27
W35	28	29	30	31			

AUGUST

SUNDAY | 21

MONDAY | 22

TUESDAY | 23

WEDNESDAY | 24

THURSDAY | 25

FRIDAY | 26

SATURDAY | 27

REMEMBER FOR NEXT WEEK

WRITING THIS WEEK

WEEK 34   AUGUST 21 – AUGUST 27

What I'm writing this week? And how will I measure it (words, scenes, etc)?

When will I get it done?

What do I need to make it happen?

What could keep me from reaching my goal?

How'd I do? Did I reach my goal? Exceed my goal? Miss my goal?

What can I change next week to improve my outcome?

Do I need assistance to make it happen? If so, who?

FOCUS THIS WEEK:

WEEK 35   AUGUST 28 – SEPTEMBER 3

TOP PRIORITIES   APPOINTMENTS / DEADLINES

_____   _____ / _____
_____   _____ / _____
_____   _____ / _____
_____   _____ / _____
_____   _____ / _____
_____   _____ / _____

WRITING:

_____
_____
_____
_____
_____
_____
_____
_____
_____

MARKETING   NOTES

_____   _____
_____   _____
_____   _____
_____   _____
_____   _____
_____   _____

LIST SOMETHING GOOD FROM THIS WEEK.   LIST HOW YOU CAN MAKE NEXT WEEK BETTER.

	SU	MO	TU	WE	TH	FR	SA
W31		1	2	3	4	5	6
W32	7	8	9	10	11	12	13
W33	14	15	16	17	18	19	20
W34	21	22	23	24	25	26	27
W35	28	29	30	31	1	2	3

AUGUST

SUNDAY | 28

MONDAY | 29

TUESDAY | 30

WEDNESDAY | 31

THURSDAY | 01

FRIDAY | 02

SATURDAY | 03

REMEMBER FOR NEXT WEEK

WRITING THIS WEEK

WEEK 35   AUGUST 28 – SEPTEMBER 3

What I'm writing this week? And how will I measure it (words, scenes, etc)?

When will I get it done?

What do I need to make it happen?

What could keep me from reaching my goal?

How'd I do? Did I reach my goal? Exceed my goal? Miss my goal?

What can I change next week to improve my outcome?

Do I need assistance to make it happen? If so, who?

AUGUST
REVIEW

MY GOALS FOR THIS MONTH:
_____
_____
_____
_____
_____
_____

THIS MONTH I ACHIEVED:
_____
_____
_____
_____
_____

WHAT WORKED:
_____
_____
_____
_____
_____

WHAT DIDN'T WORK:
_____
_____
_____
_____

DO MORE OF:	DO LESS OF:
_____	_____
_____	_____
_____	_____
_____	_____
_____	_____

INCOME TRACKER

GOAL FOR THIS MONTH	I ACHIEVED

Date	Source	Description	Amount
		TOTAL INCOME	

EXPENSE TRACKER

GOAL FOR THIS MONTH	I ACHIEVED

Date	Category	Description	Amount
	TOTAL EXPENSES		

...my story matters.

SEPTEMBER 2022

SEPTEMBER
2022

FOCUS:

NOTES	SUNDAY	MONDAY	TUESDAY
	WEEK 35		
	4 WEEK 36	5	6
	11 WEEK 37	12	13
	18 WEEK 38	19	20
	25 WEEK 39	26	27

	SU MO TU WE TH FR SA		SU MO TU WE TH FR SA
AUGUST	W31 1 2 3 4 5 6	OCTOBER	W39 1
	W32 7 8 9 10 11 12 13		W40 2 3 4 5 6 7 8
	W33 14 15 16 17 18 19 20		W41 9 10 11 12 13 14 15
	W34 21 22 23 24 25 26 27		W42 16 17 18 19 20 21 22
	W35 28 29 30 31		W43 23 24 25 26 27 28 29
			W44 30 31

WEDNESDAY	THURSDAY	FRIDAY	SATURDAY
	1	2	3
7	8	9	10
14	15	16	17
21	22	23	24
28	29	30	

SEPTEMBER
OVERVIEW

FOCUS:

REMINDERS

GOAL

_____
_____
_____
_____
_____

GOAL

_____
_____
_____
_____
_____

THINGS TO REMEMBER

- [ ] _____
- [ ] _____
- [ ] _____
- [ ] _____
- [ ] _____
- [ ] _____
- [ ] _____
- [ ] _____
- [ ] _____
- [ ] _____
- [ ] _____
- [ ] _____

GOAL

_____
_____
_____
_____
_____

GOAL

_____
_____
_____
_____
_____

Master To Do List

- [ ]
- [ ]   Due Date
- [ ]   Due Date
- [ ]   Due Date
- [ ]   Due Date
- [ ]   Due Date
- [ ]   Due Date
- [ ]   Due Date
- [ ]   Due Date
- [ ]   Due Date
- [ ]   Due Date
- [ ]   Due Date
- [ ]   Due Date
- [ ]   Due Date
- [ ]   Due Date
- [ ]   Due Date
- [ ]   Due Date
- [ ]   Due Date
- [ ]   Due Date
- [ ]   Due Date
- [ ]   Due Date
- [ ]   Due Date
- [ ]   Due Date
- [ ]   Due Date

WORD COUNT TRACKER

GOAL FOR THIS MONTH	I ACHIEVED

YEAR TO DATE: _____

FOCUS THIS WEEK:

WEEK 36 SEPTEMBER 4 – SEPTEMBER 10

TOP PRIORITIES APPOINTMENTS / DEADLINES

/
/
/
/
/
/

WRITING:

MARKETING NOTES

LIST SOMETHING GOOD FROM THIS WEEK. LIST HOW YOU CAN MAKE NEXT WEEK BETTER.

SEPTEMBER

	SU	MO	TU	WE	TH	FR	SA
W35					1	2	3
W36	4	5	6	7	8	9	10
W37	11	12	13	14	15	16	17
W38	18	19	20	21	22	23	24
W39	25	26	27	28	29	30	

SUNDAY | 04

MONDAY | 05

TUESDAY | 06

WEDNESDAY | 07

THURSDAY | 08

FRIDAY | 09

SATURDAY | 10

REMEMBER FOR NEXT WEEK

WRITING THIS WEEK

WEEK 36   SEPTEMBER 4 - SEPTEMBER 10

What I'm writing this week? And how will I measure it (words, scenes, etc)?

When will I get it done?

What do I need to make it happen?

What could keep me from reaching my goal?

How'd I do? Did I reach my goal? Exceed my goal? Miss my goal?

What can I change next week to improve my outcome?

Do I need assistance to make it happen? If so, who?

FOCUS THIS WEEK:

WEEK 37 SEPTEMBER 11 – SEPTEMBER 17

TOP PRIORITIES

APPOINTMENTS / DEADLINES

/
/
/
/
/
/

WRITING:

MARKETING

NOTES

LIST SOMETHING GOOD FROM THIS WEEK.

LIST HOW YOU CAN MAKE NEXT WEEK BETTER.

SEPTEMBER

	SU	MO	TU	WE	TH	FR	SA
W35						1	2	3
W36	4	5	6	7	8	9	10
W37	11	12	13	14	15	16	17
W38	18	19	20	21	22	23	24
W39	25	26	27	28	29	30	

SUNDAY | 11

MONDAY | 12

TUESDAY | 13

WEDNESDAY | 14

THURSDAY | 15

FRIDAY | 16

SATURDAY | 17

REMEMBER FOR NEXT WEEK

WRITING THIS WEEK

WEEK 37   SEPTEMBER 11 – SEPTEMBER 17

What I'm writing this week? And how will I measure it (words, scenes, etc)?

When will I get it done?

What do I need to make it happen?

What could keep me from reaching my goal?

How'd I do? Did I reach my goal? Exceed my goal? Miss my goal?

What can I change next week to improve my outcome?

Do I need assistance to make it happen? If so, who?

FOCUS THIS WEEK:

WEEK 38 SEPTEMBER 18 – SEPTEMBER 24

TOP PRIORITIES APPOINTMENTS / DEADLINES

/
/
/
/
/
/

WRITING:

MARKETING NOTES

LIST SOMETHING GOOD FROM THIS WEEK. LIST HOW YOU CAN MAKE NEXT WEEK BETTER.

SEPTEMBER

	SU	MO	TU	WE	TH	FR	SA
W35					1	2	3
W36	4	5	6	7	8	9	10
W37	11	12	13	14	15	16	17
W38	18	19	20	21	22	23	24
W39	25	26	27	28	29	30	

SUNDAY | 18

MONDAY | 19

TUESDAY | 20

WEDNESDAY | 21

THURSDAY | 22

FRIDAY | 23

SATURDAY | 24

REMEMBER FOR NEXT WEEK

WRITING THIS WEEK

WEEK 38 SEPTEMBER 18 – SEPTEMBER 24

What I'm writing this week? And how will I measure it (words, scenes, etc)?

When will I get it done?

What do I need to make it happen?

What could keep me from reaching my goal?

How'd I do? Did I reach my goal? Exceed my goal? Miss my goal?

What can I change next week to improve my outcome?

Do I need assistance to make it happen? If so, who?

FOCUS THIS WEEK:

WEEK 39　　　　　　　　　　　　　　　　　　　　　　　SEPTEMBER 25 – OCTOBER 1

TOP PRIORITIES　　　APPOINTMENTS / DEADLINES

　　　／
　　　／
　　　／
　　　／
　　　／
　　　／

WRITING:

MARKETING　　　　　　　　　　　　NOTES

LIST SOMETHING GOOD FROM THIS WEEK.　　　LIST HOW YOU CAN MAKE NEXT WEEK BETTER.

	SU	MO	TU	WE	TH	FR	SA
W35						1	2	3
W36	4	5	6	7	8	9	10
W37	11	12	13	14	15	16	17
W38	18	19	20	21	22	23	24
W39	25	26	27	28	29	30	1

SEPTEMBER

SUNDAY | 25

MONDAY | 26

TUESDAY | 27

WEDNESDAY | 28

THURSDAY | 29

FRIDAY | 30

SATURDAY | 01

REMEMBER FOR NEXT WEEK

WRITING THIS WEEK

WEEK 39   SEPTEMBER 25 - OCTOBER 1

What I'm writing this week? And how will I measure it (words, scenes, etc)?

When will I get it done?

What do I need to make it happen?

What could keep me from reaching my goal?

How'd I do? Did I reach my goal? Exceed my goal? Miss my goal?

What can I change next week to improve my outcome?

Do I need assistance to make it happen? If so, who?

SEPTEMBER
REVIEW

MY GOALS FOR THIS MONTH:
_____
_____
_____
_____
_____

THIS MONTH I ACHIEVED:
_____
_____
_____
_____

WHAT WORKED:
_____
_____
_____
_____

WHAT DIDN'T WORK:
_____
_____
_____
_____

DO MORE OF:	DO LESS OF:
_____	_____
_____	_____
_____	_____
_____	_____
_____	_____

INCOME TRACKER

GOAL FOR THIS MONTH	I ACHIEVED

Date	Source	Description	Amount
		TOTAL INCOME	

EXPENSE TRACKER

GOAL FOR THIS MONTH	I ACHIEVED

Date	Category	Description	Amount
		TOTAL EXPENSES	

...my story matters.

OCTOBER 2022

OCTOBER
2022

FOCUS:

NOTES	SUNDAY	MONDAY	TUESDAY
	WEEK 39		
	2 WEEK 40	3	4
	9 WEEK 41	10	11
	16 WEEK 42	17	18
	23 / 30 WEEK 43	24 / 31	25

	SEPTEMBER							NOVEMBER						
		SU	MO	TU	WE	TH	FR	SA	SU	MO	TU	WE	TH	FR	SA

SEPTEMBER
W35   1   2   3
W36 4   5   6   7   8   9 10
W37 11 12 13 14 15 16 17
W38 18 19 20 21 22 23 24
W39 25 26 27 28 29 30

NOVEMBER
W44   1   2   3   4   5
W45 6   7   8   9 10 11 12
W46 13 14 15 16 17 18 19
W47 20 21 22 23 24 25 26
W48 27 28 29 30

WEDNESDAY	THURSDAY	FRIDAY	SATURDAY
			1
5	6	7	8
12	13	14	15
19	20	21	22
26	27	28	29

OCTOBER
OVERVIEW

FOCUS:

REMINDERS

GOAL

GOAL

GOAL

THINGS TO REMEMBER

- ☐
- ☐
- ☐
- ☐
- ☐
- ☐
- ☐
- ☐
- ☐
- ☐
- ☐
- ☐

GOAL

Master To Do List

- [ ]
- [ ]   Due Date
- [ ]   Due Date
- [ ]   Due Date
- [ ]   Due Date
- [ ]   Due Date
- [ ]   Due Date
- [ ]   Due Date
- [ ]   Due Date
- [ ]   Due Date
- [ ]   Due Date
- [ ]   Due Date
- [ ]   Due Date
- [ ]   Due Date
- [ ]   Due Date
- [ ]   Due Date
- [ ]   Due Date
- [ ]   Due Date
- [ ]   Due Date
- [ ]   Due Date
- [ ]   Due Date
- [ ]   Due Date
- [ ]   Due Date
- [ ]   Due Date
- [ ]   Due Date
- [ ]   Due Date

Due Date

WORD COUNT TRACKER

GOAL FOR THIS MONTH	I ACHIEVED

YEAR TO DATE: _____

FOCUS THIS WEEK:

WEEK 40   OCTOBER 2 – OCTOBER 8

TOP PRIORITIES   APPOINTMENTS / DEADLINES

_____   /
_____   /
_____   /
_____   /
_____   /
_____   /

WRITING:

_____
_____
_____
_____
_____
_____
_____

MARKETING   NOTES

_____   _____
_____   _____
_____   _____
_____   _____
_____   _____

LIST SOMETHING GOOD FROM THIS WEEK.   LIST HOW YOU CAN MAKE NEXT WEEK BETTER.

	SU	MO	TU	WE	TH	FR	SA
W39							1
W40	2	3	4	5	6	7	8
W41	9	10	11	12	13	14	15
W42	16	17	18	19	20	21	22
W43	23	24	25	26	27	28	29
W44	30	31					

OCTOBER

SUNDAY | 02

MONDAY | 03

TUESDAY | 04

WEDNESDAY | 05

THURSDAY | 06

FRIDAY | 07

SATURDAY | 08

REMEMBER FOR NEXT WEEK

WRITING THIS WEEK

WEEK 40   OCTOBER 2 - OCTOBER 8

What I'm writing this week? And how will I measure it (words, scenes, etc)?

When will I get it done?

What do I need to make it happen?

What could keep me from reaching my goal?

How'd I do? Did I reach my goal? Exceed my goal? Miss my goal?

What can I change next week to improve my outcome?

Do I need assistance to make it happen? If so, who?

FOCUS THIS WEEK:

WEEK 41 OCTOBER 9 – OCTOBER 15

TOP PRIORITIES APPOINTMENTS / DEADLINES

/
/
/
/
/
/

WRITING:

MARKETING NOTES

LIST SOMETHING GOOD FROM THIS WEEK. LIST HOW YOU CAN MAKE NEXT WEEK BETTER.

	SU	MO	TU	WE	TH	FR	SA
W39							1
W40	2	3	4	5	6	7	8
W41	9	10	11	12	13	14	15
W42	16	17	18	19	20	21	22
W43	23	24	25	26	27	28	29
W44	30	31					

OCTOBER

SUNDAY | 09

MONDAY | 10

TUESDAY | 11

WEDNESDAY | 12

THURSDAY | 13

FRIDAY | 14

SATURDAY | 15

REMEMBER FOR NEXT WEEK

WRITING THIS WEEK

WEEK 41   OCTOBER 9 – OCTOBER 15

What I'm writing this week? And how will I measure it (words, scenes, etc)?

When will I get it done?

What do I need to make it happen?

What could keep me from reaching my goal?

How'd I do? Did I reach my goal? Exceed my goal? Miss my goal?

What can I change next week to improve my outcome?

Do I need assistance to make it happen? If so, who?

FOCUS THIS WEEK:

WEEK 42 OCTOBER 16 – OCTOBER 22

TOP PRIORITIES APPOINTMENTS / DEADLINES

/
/
/
/
/
/

WRITING:

MARKETING NOTES

LIST SOMETHING GOOD FROM THIS WEEK. LIST HOW YOU CAN MAKE NEXT WEEK BETTER.

	SU	MO	TU	WE	TH	FR	SA
W39							1
W40	2	3	4	5	6	7	8
W41	9	10	11	12	13	14	15
W42	16	17	18	19	20	21	22
W43	23	24	25	26	27	28	29
W44	30	31					

OCTOBER

SUNDAY | 16

MONDAY | 17

TUESDAY | 18

WEDNESDAY | 19

THURSDAY | 20

FRIDAY | 21

SATURDAY | 22

REMEMBER FOR NEXT WEEK

WRITING THIS WEEK

WEEK 42   OCTOBER 16 – OCTOBER 22

What I'm writing this week? And how will I measure it (words, scenes, etc)?

When will I get it done?

What do I need to make it happen?

What could keep me from reaching my goal?

How'd I do? Did I reach my goal? Exceed my goal? Miss my goal?

What can I change next week to improve my outcome?

Do I need assistance to make it happen? If so, who?

FOCUS THIS WEEK:

WEEK 43　　　　　　　　　　　　　　　　　　　　　　　　　OCTOBER 23 – OCTOBER 29

TOP PRIORITIES　　　　　　APPOINTMENTS / DEADLINES

_____　　　／ _____
_____　　　／ _____
_____　　　／ _____
_____　　　／ _____
_____　　　／ _____
_____　　　／ _____

WRITING:

_____
_____
_____
_____
_____
_____
_____
_____

MARKETING　　　　　　　　　　　　　NOTES

_____　　　_____
_____　　　_____
_____　　　_____
_____　　　_____
_____　　　_____
_____　　　_____

LIST SOMETHING GOOD FROM THIS WEEK.　　　LIST HOW YOU CAN MAKE NEXT WEEK BETTER.

	SU	MO	TU	WE	TH	FR	SA
W39							1
W40	2	3	4	5	6	7	8
W41	9	10	11	12	13	14	15
W42	16	17	18	19	20	21	22
W43	23	24	25	26	27	28	29
W44	30	31					

OCTOBER

SUNDAY | 23

MONDAY | 24

TUESDAY | 25

WEDNESDAY | 26

THURSDAY | 27

FRIDAY | 28

SATURDAY | 29

REMEMBER FOR NEXT WEEK

WRITING THIS WEEK

WEEK 43   OCTOBER 23 – OCTOBER 29

What I'm writing this week? And how will I measure it (words, scenes, etc)?

When will I get it done?

What do I need to make it happen?

What could keep me from reaching my goal?

How'd I do? Did I reach my goal? Exceed my goal? Miss my goal?

What can I change next week to improve my outcome?

Do I need assistance to make it happen? If so, who?

OCTOBER

REVIEW

MY GOALS FOR THIS MONTH:
_____
_____
_____
_____
_____
_____

THIS MONTH I ACHIEVED:
_____
_____
_____
_____
_____

WHAT WORKED:
_____
_____
_____
_____
_____

WHAT DIDN'T WORK:
_____
_____
_____
_____

DO MORE OF:	DO LESS OF:
_____	_____
_____	_____
_____	_____
_____	_____
_____	_____

INCOME TRACKER

GOAL FOR THIS MONTH	I ACHIEVED

Date	Source	Description	Amount
		TOTAL INCOME	

EXPENSE TRACKER

GOAL FOR THIS MONTH	I ACHIEVED

Date	Category	Description	Amount
	TOTAL EXPENSES		

...my story matters.

NOVEMBER 2022

NOVEMBER
2022

FOCUS:

NOTES	SUNDAY	MONDAY	TUESDAY
	WEEK 44		1
	6 WEEK 45	7	8
	13 WEEK 46	14	15
	20 WEEK 47	21	22
	27 WEEK 48	28	29

OCTOBER

SU	MO	TU	WE	TH	FR	SA
W39						1
W40 2	3	4	5	6	7	8
W41 9	10	11	12	13	14	15
W42 16	17	18	19	20	21	22
W43 23	24	25	26	27	28	29
W44 30	31					

DECEMBER

SU	MO	TU	WE	TH	FR	SA
W48					1	2	3
W49 4	5	6	7	8	9	10
W50 11	12	13	14	15	16	17
W51 18	19	20	21	22	23	24
W52 25	26	27	28	29	30	31

WEDNESDAY	THURSDAY	FRIDAY	SATURDAY
2	3	4	5
9	10	11	12
16	17	18	19
23	24	25	26
30			

NOVEMBER
OVERVIEW

FOCUS:

REMINDERS

GOAL

GOAL

GOAL

GOAL

THINGS TO REMEMBER

Master To Do List

	Due Date
☐	
☐	Due Date
☐	Due Date
☐	Due Date
☐	Due Date
☐	Due Date
☐	Due Date
☐	Due Date
☐	Due Date
☐	Due Date
☐	Due Date
☐	Due Date
☐	Due Date
☐	Due Date
☐	Due Date
☐	Due Date
☐	Due Date
☐	Due Date
☐	Due Date
☐	Due Date
☐	Due Date
☐	Due Date
☐	Due Date
☐	Due Date
	Due Date

WORD COUNT TRACKER

GOAL FOR THIS MONTH	I ACHIEVED

YEAR TO DATE: _____

FOCUS THIS WEEK:

WEEK 44   OCTOBER 30 – NOVEMBER 5

| TOP PRIORITIES | APPOINTMENTS / DEADLINES |

WRITING:

| MARKETING | NOTES |

LIST SOMETHING GOOD FROM THIS WEEK.   LIST HOW YOU CAN MAKE NEXT WEEK BETTER.

	SU	MO	TU	WE	TH	FR	SA
W44	30	31	1	2	3	4	5
W45	6	7	8	9	10	11	12
W46	13	14	15	16	17	18	19
W47	20	21	22	23	24	25	26
W48	27	28	29	30			

NOVEMBER

SUNDAY | 30

MONDAY | 31

TUESDAY | 01

WEDNESDAY | 02

THURSDAY | 03

FRIDAY | 04

SATURDAY | 05

REMEMBER FOR NEXT WEEK

WRITING THIS WEEK

WEEK 44　　　　　　　　　　　　　　　　　　　　　　　　　　　　　　　OCTOBER 30 - NOVEMBER 5

What I'm writing this week? And how will I measure it (words, scenes, etc)?

When will I get it done?

What do I need to make it happen?

What could keep me from reaching my goal?

How'd I do? Did I reach my goal? Exceed my goal? Miss my goal?

What can I change next week to improve my outcome?

Do I need assistance to make it happen? If so, who?

FOCUS THIS WEEK:

WEEK 45   NOVEMBER 6 – NOVEMBER 12

TOP PRIORITIES   APPOINTMENTS / DEADLINES

_____   _____ / _____
_____   _____ / _____
_____   _____ / _____
_____   _____ / _____
_____   _____ / _____
_____   _____ / _____

WRITING:

_____
_____
_____
_____
_____
_____
_____
_____

MARKETING   NOTES

_____   _____
_____   _____
_____   _____
_____   _____
_____   _____
_____   _____

LIST SOMETHING GOOD FROM THIS WEEK.   LIST HOW YOU CAN MAKE NEXT WEEK BETTER.

	SU	MO	TU	WE	TH	FR	SA
W44			1	2	3	4	5
W45	6	7	8	9	10	11	12
W46	13	14	15	16	17	18	19
W47	20	21	22	23	24	25	26
W48	27	28	29	30			

NOVEMBER

SUNDAY | 06

MONDAY | 07

TUESDAY | 08

WEDNESDAY | 09

THURSDAY | 10

FRIDAY | 11

SATURDAY | 12

REMEMBER FOR NEXT WEEK

WRITING THIS WEEK

WEEK 45   NOVEMBER 6 – NOVEMBER 12

What I'm writing this week? And how will I measure it (words, scenes, etc)?

When will I get it done?

What do I need to make it happen?

What could keep me from reaching my goal?

How'd I do? Did I reach my goal? Exceed my goal? Miss my goal?

What can I change next week to improve my outcome?

Do I need assistance to make it happen? If so, who?

FOCUS THIS WEEK:

WEEK 46 NOVEMBER 13 – NOVEMBER 19

TOP PRIORITIES APPOINTMENTS / DEADLINES

/
/
/
/
/
/

WRITING:

MARKETING NOTES

LIST SOMETHING GOOD FROM THIS WEEK. LIST HOW YOU CAN MAKE NEXT WEEK BETTER.

	SU	MO	TU	WE	TH	FR	SA
W44			1	2	3	4	5
W45	6	7	8	9	10	11	12
W46	13	14	15	16	17	18	19
W47	20	21	22	23	24	25	26
W48	27	28	29	30			

NOVEMBER

SUNDAY | 13

MONDAY | 14

TUESDAY | 15

WEDNESDAY | 16

THURSDAY | 17

FRIDAY | 18

SATURDAY | 19

REMEMBER FOR NEXT WEEK

WRITING THIS WEEK

WEEK 46   NOVEMBER 13 – NOVEMBER 19

What I'm writing this week? And how will I measure it (words, scenes, etc)?

When will I get it done?

What do I need to make it happen?

What could keep me from reaching my goal?

How'd I do? Did I reach my goal? Exceed my goal? Miss my goal?

What can I change next week to improve my outcome?

Do I need assistance to make it happen? If so, who?

FOCUS THIS WEEK:

WEEK 47 NOVEMBER 20 – NOVEMBER 26

TOP PRIORITIES   APPOINTMENTS / DEADLINES

/
/
/
/
/
/

WRITING:

MARKETING   NOTES

LIST SOMETHING GOOD FROM THIS WEEK.   LIST HOW YOU CAN MAKE NEXT WEEK BETTER.

	SU	MO	TU	WE	TH	FR	SA
W44			1	2	3	4	5
W45	6	7	8	9	10	11	12
W46	13	14	15	16	17	18	19
W47	20	21	22	23	24	25	26
W48	27	28	29	30			

NOVEMBER

SUNDAY | 20

MONDAY | 21

TUESDAY | 22

WEDNESDAY | 23

THURSDAY | 24

FRIDAY | 25

SATURDAY | 26

REMEMBER FOR NEXT WEEK

WRITING THIS WEEK

WEEK 47 NOVEMBER 20 – NOVEMBER 26

What I'm writing this week? And how will I measure it (words, scenes, etc)?

When will I get it done?

What do I need to make it happen?

What could keep me from reaching my goal?

How'd I do? Did I reach my goal? Exceed my goal? Miss my goal?

What can I change next week to improve my outcome?

Do I need assistance to make it happen? If so, who?

FOCUS THIS WEEK:

WEEK 48   NOVEMBER 27 - DECEMBER 3

TOP PRIORITIES	APPOINTMENTS / DEADLINES
	/
	/
	/
	/
	/
	/

WRITING:

MARKETING

NOTES

LIST SOMETHING GOOD FROM THIS WEEK.   LIST HOW YOU CAN MAKE NEXT WEEK BETTER.

	SU	MO	TU	WE	TH	FR	SA
W44			1	2	3	4	5
W45	6	7	8	9	10	11	12
W46	13	14	15	16	17	18	19
W47	20	21	22	23	24	25	26
W48	27	28	29	30	1	2	3

NOVEMBER

SUNDAY | 27

MONDAY | 28

TUESDAY | 29

WEDNESDAY | 30

THURSDAY | 01

FRIDAY | 02

SATURDAY | 03

REMEMBER FOR NEXT WEEK

WRITING THIS WEEK

WEEK 48　　　　　　　　　　　　　　　　　　　　　　　　　　　　　　NOVEMBER 27 – DECEMBER 3

What I'm writing this week? And how will I measure it (words, scenes, etc)?

When will I get it done?

What do I need to make it happen?

What could keep me from reaching my goal?

How'd I do? Did I reach my goal? Exceed my goal? Miss my goal?

What can I change next week to improve my outcome?

Do I need assistance to make it happen? If so, who?

NOVEMBER
REVIEW

MY GOALS FOR THIS MONTH:
___

THIS MONTH I ACHIEVED:
___

WHAT WORKED:
___

WHAT DIDN'T WORK:
___

DO MORE OF:
___

DO LESS OF:
___

INCOME TRACKER

GOAL FOR THIS MONTH	I ACHIEVED

Date	Source	Description	Amount
	TOTAL INCOME		

EXPENSE TRACKER

GOAL FOR THIS MONTH	I ACHIEVED

Date	Category	Description	Amount
	TOTAL EXPENSES		

...my story matters.

DECEMBER 2022

DECEMBER
2022

FOCUS:

NOTES	SUNDAY	MONDAY	TUESDAY
	WEEK 48		
	4 / WEEK 49	5	6
	11 / WEEK 50	12	13
	18 / WEEK 51	19	20
	25 / WEEK 52	26	27

	NOVEMBER							JANUARY						
	SU	MO	TU	WE	TH	FR	SA	SU	MO	TU	WE	TH	FR	SA
W44 / W53			1	2	3	4	5							1
W45 / W1	6	7	8	9	10	11	12	2	3	4	5	6	7	8
W46 / W2	13	14	15	16	17	18	19	9	10	11	12	13	14	15
W47 / W3	20	21	22	23	24	25	26	16	17	18	19	20	21	22
W48 / W4	27	28	29	30				23	24	25	26	27	28	29
W5								30	31					

WEDNESDAY	THURSDAY	FRIDAY	SATURDAY
	1	2	3
7	8	9	10
14	15	16	17
21	22	23	24
28	29	30	31

DECEMBER OVERVIEW

FOCUS:

REMINDERS

GOAL

GOAL

GOAL

GOAL

THINGS TO REMEMBER

- [ ]
- [ ]
- [ ]
- [ ]
- [ ]
- [ ]
- [ ]
- [ ]
- [ ]
- [ ]
- [ ]
- [ ]

Master To Do List

☐

☐ _____ Due Date

☐ _____ Due Date

☐ _____ Due Date

☐ _____ Due Date

☐ _____ Due Date

☐ _____ Due Date

☐ _____ Due Date

☐ _____ Due Date

☐ _____ Due Date

☐ _____ Due Date

☐ _____ Due Date

☐ _____ Due Date

☐ _____ Due Date

☐ _____ Due Date

☐ _____ Due Date

☐ _____ Due Date

☐ _____ Due Date

☐ _____ Due Date

☐ _____ Due Date

☐ _____ Due Date

☐ _____ Due Date

☐ _____ Due Date

☐ _____ Due Date

☐ _____ Due Date

WORD COUNT TRACKER

GOAL FOR THIS MONTH	I ACHIEVED

YEAR TO DATE: _____

FOCUS THIS WEEK:

WEEK 49   DECEMBER 4 – DECEMBER 10

TOP PRIORITIES

APPOINTMENTS / DEADLINES

/
/
/
/
/
/

WRITING:

MARKETING

NOTES

LIST SOMETHING GOOD FROM THIS WEEK.

LIST HOW YOU CAN MAKE NEXT WEEK BETTER.

	SU	MO	TU	WE	TH	FR	SA
W48					1	2	3
W49	4	5	6	7	8	9	10
W50	11	12	13	14	15	16	17
W51	18	19	20	21	22	23	24
W52	25	26	27	28	29	30	31

DECEMBER

SUNDAY | 04

MONDAY | 05

TUESDAY | 06

WEDNESDAY | 07

THURSDAY | 08

FRIDAY | 09

SATURDAY | 10

REMEMBER FOR NEXT WEEK

WRITING THIS WEEK

WEEK 49   DECEMBER 4 – DECEMBER 10

What I'm writing this week? And how will I measure it (words, scenes, etc)?

When will I get it done?

What do I need to make it happen?

What could keep me from reaching my goal?

How'd I do? Did I reach my goal? Exceed my goal? Miss my goal?

What can I change next week to improve my outcome?

Do I need assistance to make it happen? If so, who?

FOCUS THIS WEEK:

WEEK 50   DECEMBER 11 – DECEMBER 17

TOP PRIORITIES   APPOINTMENTS / DEADLINES

_____   ____ / _____
_____   ____ / _____
_____   ____ / _____
_____   ____ / _____
_____   ____ / _____
_____   ____ / _____

WRITING:

_____
_____
_____
_____
_____
_____
_____

MARKETING   NOTES

_____   _____
_____   _____
_____   _____
_____   _____
_____   _____
_____   _____

LIST SOMETHING GOOD FROM THIS WEEK.   LIST HOW YOU CAN MAKE NEXT WEEK BETTER.

	SU	MO	TU	WE	TH	FR	SA
W48						1	2	3
W49	4	5	6	7	8	9	10
W50	11	12	13	14	15	16	17
W51	18	19	20	21	22	23	24
W52	25	26	27	28	29	30	31

DECEMBER

SUNDAY | 11

MONDAY | 12

TUESDAY | 13

WEDNESDAY | 14

THURSDAY | 15

FRIDAY | 16

SATURDAY | 17

REMEMBER FOR NEXT WEEK

WRITING THIS WEEK

WEEK 50 DECEMBER 11 – DECEMBER 17

What I'm writing this week? And how will I measure it (words, scenes, etc)?

When will I get it done?

What do I need to make it happen?

What could keep me from reaching my goal?

How'd I do? Did I reach my goal? Exceed my goal? Miss my goal?

What can I change next week to improve my outcome?

Do I need assistance to make it happen? If so, who?

FOCUS THIS WEEK:

WEEK 51 DECEMBER 18 – DECEMBER 24

TOP PRIORITIES APPOINTMENTS / DEADLINES

/
/
/
/
/
/

WRITING:

MARKETING NOTES

LIST SOMETHING GOOD FROM THIS WEEK. LIST HOW YOU CAN MAKE NEXT WEEK BETTER.

	SU	MO	TU	WE	TH	FR	SA
W48					1	2	3
W49	4	5	6	7	8	9	10
W50	11	12	13	14	15	16	17
W51	18	19	20	21	22	23	24
W52	25	26	27	28	29	30	31

DECEMBER

SUNDAY | 18

MONDAY | 19

TUESDAY | 20

WEDNESDAY | 21

THURSDAY | 22

FRIDAY | 23

SATURDAY | 24

REMEMBER FOR NEXT WEEK

WRITING THIS WEEK

WEEK 51								DECEMBER 18 - DECEMBER 24

What I'm writing this week? And how will I measure it (words, scenes, etc)?

When will I get it done?

What do I need to make it happen?

What could keep me from reaching my goal?

How'd I do? Did I reach my goal? Exceed my goal? Miss my goal?

What can I change next week to improve my outcome?

Do I need assistance to make it happen? If so, who?

FOCUS THIS WEEK:

WEEK 52   DECEMBER 25 – DECEMBER 31

TOP PRIORITIES	APPOINTMENTS / DEADLINES
_____	_____ / _____
_____	_____ / _____
_____	_____ / _____
_____	_____ / _____
_____	_____ / _____
_____	_____ / _____

WRITING:

_____
_____
_____
_____
_____
_____
_____
_____

MARKETING	NOTES
_____	_____
_____	_____
_____	_____
_____	_____
_____	_____

LIST SOMETHING GOOD FROM THIS WEEK.   LIST HOW YOU CAN MAKE NEXT WEEK BETTER.

	SU	MO	TU	WE	TH	FR	SA
W48					1	2	3
W49	4	5	6	7	8	9	10
W50	11	12	13	14	15	16	17
W51	18	19	20	21	22	23	24
W52	25	26	27	28	29	30	31

DECEMBER

SUNDAY | 25

MONDAY | 26

TUESDAY | 27

WEDNESDAY | 28

THURSDAY | 29

FRIDAY | 30

SATURDAY | 31

REMEMBER FOR NEXT WEEK

WRITING THIS WEEK

WEEK 52   DECEMBER 25 – DECEMBER 31

What I'm writing this week? And how will I measure it (words, scenes, etc)?

When will I get it done?

What do I need to make it happen?

What could keep me from reaching my goal?

How'd I do? Did I reach my goal? Exceed my goal? Miss my goal?

What can I change next week to improve my outcome?

Do I need assistance to make it happen? If so, who?

DECEMBER
REVIEW

MY GOALS FOR THIS MONTH:
___
___
___
___
___
___

THIS MONTH I ACHIEVED:
___
___
___
___
___

WHAT WORKED:
___
___
___
___
___

WHAT DIDN'T WORK:
___
___
___
___

DO MORE OF: DO LESS OF:
___   ___
___   ___
___   ___
___   ___
___   ___

INCOME TRACKER

GOAL FOR THIS MONTH	I ACHIEVED

Date	Source	Description	Amount
	TOTAL INCOME		

EXPENSE TRACKER

GOAL FOR THIS MONTH	I ACHIEVED

Date	Category	Description	Amount
		TOTAL EXPENSES	

Notes

I WRITE 2022

Your story and your voice matters. So, don't just think about your book. Write it!

— DANA PITTMAN
Chief Storyteller with Danja Tales

www.ingramcontent.com/pod-product-compliance
Lightning Source LLC
Chambersburg PA
CBHW051801100526
44592CB00016B/2520